Beating Bowel Cancer

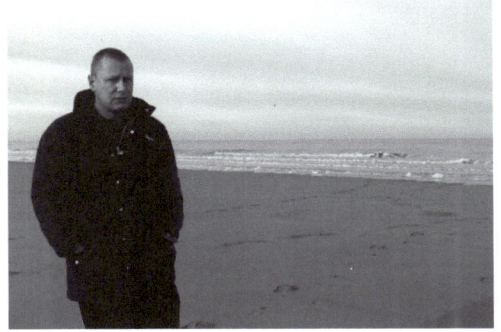

I0470792

By Tim Darvell

In April 2012 the dreaded cancer word came into our family. One minute I was sitting with my mother expecting a normal discharge from hospital, and then in the blink of an eye our world was turned upside down when we were told that mum had bowel cancer. I could probably write a whole book on that subject alone, but that is a private battle mum is going through. I wanted to do something in the way of fundraising, and after much consideration I decided that a photographic book with all proceeds going to the "Beating Bowel Cancer" charity would be something I would like to do.

My love and passion for photography is fairly recent and I only invested in a proper SLR camera in September 2011. I make no claims to be the world's best photographer, I am still a relative novice, but I am hoping that the pictures and the stories behind them in this book will bring as much enjoyment to the reader as I had taking them. My special thanks to Jo for proofreading the text and correcting the grammatical errors. My passion for photography has been ignited by Jules, and without her encouragement, support and photographic camaraderie this book simply would not have been written.

This book will feature photos on various subjects, ideas and technical approaches. Over the last year I have been busy taking pictures and learning different techniques, and my joint photographic blog "Two Views" http://twoviewsphotographic.blogspot.com/plays a pivotal role as the driving force behind this book as does my co-conspirator on that blog "The Brunette". The question we ask ourselves is, "How can we continue to push our photographic boundaries in terms of technical knowledge, new challenges and creativity and have fun at the same time?"

Contents

1) Portrait

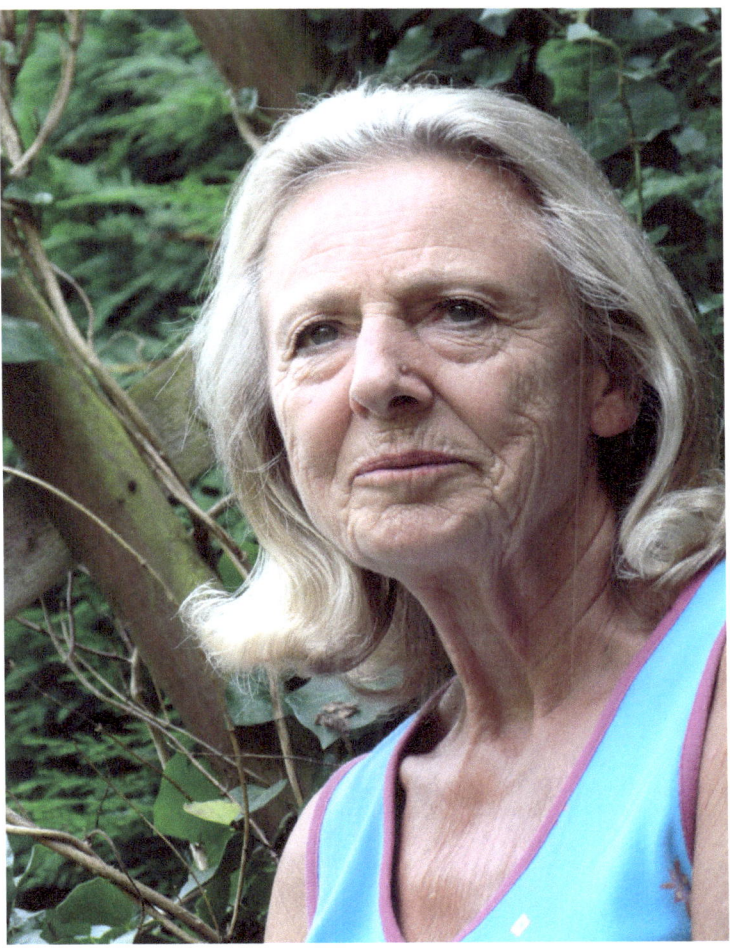

Portrait photography is something I probably feel least comfortable with when it comes to taking photos, as there is an air of expectation of high quality photos if you specifically get people to pose for you. I have found that the best portrait photos I have managed to take have been when the subject is unaware of the camera, and the photograph is taken in a natural environment.

The subject of this portrait is my mother whose fight against bowel cancer is also the inspiration for the book so it seems like a good place to start. The photo was taken in my sister's garden in Alvescot. There was no time consuming setting the scene involved or posing for the camera as mum was blissfully unaware of the picture being taken. I achieved the low angle by lying on the grass with mum sitting on a wooden bench, and although only subtle I think this angle adds to the photo. We all have numerous photos of family, but I was particularly pleased with this photo of my mother, all the more so as it was taken just a few days before she went into hospital to have major surgery to remove the cancerous tumour in her bowel. The picture therefore takes on extra significance, but also for me it is just a wonderful photo capturing a lovely happy content look in her face. As a viewer I want to know why she was looking so happy. We were at my niece's, mum's granddaughter's 6th birthday celebration and as per usual Anna was a source of amusement and entertainment no doubt contributing to the smile in no small way.

2) Skyscape

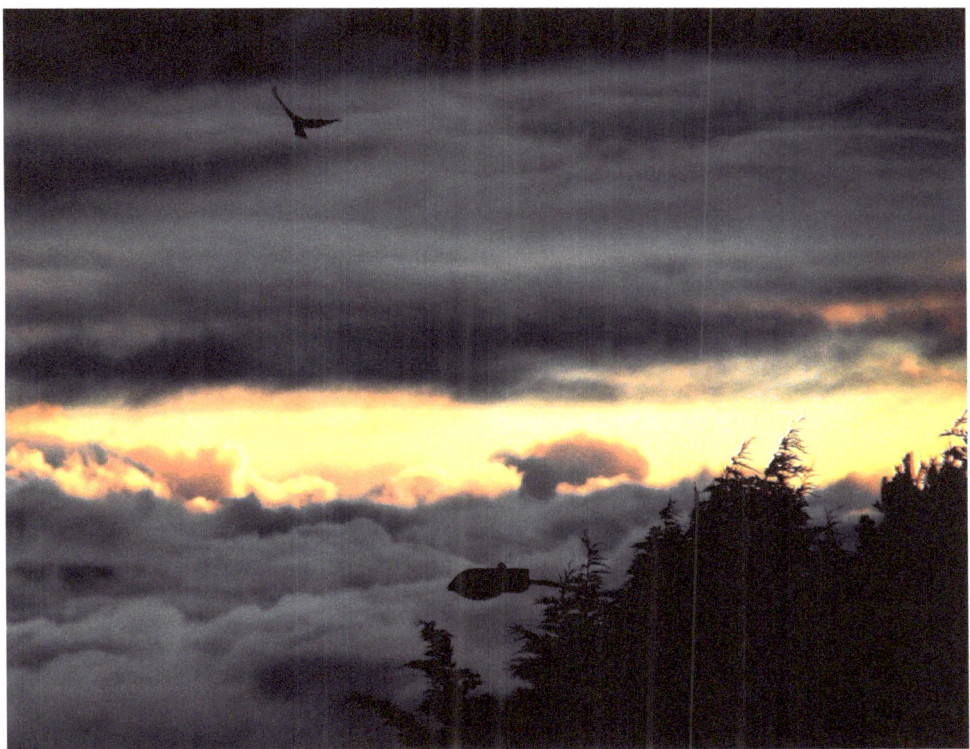

The wonderful thing about photographing the sky is that it changes pretty much every minute of every day, and you don't have to travel to exotic locations to capture a beautiful scene. I got this shot as I was driving back to my house in Reading towards the end of yet another rainy day in summer 2012. A hosepipe ban at Easter signalled the start of rain, rain and yet more rain! One of the fringe benefits of the awful weather is being blessed with some pretty spectacular skyscapes when gaps in the rain clouds allow the sun to try and burst through.

I saw this scene at sunset for quite a few miles and was deciding where I could pull over and get a decent shot of it as I wasn't sure how long the scene would last. Fortunately I tend to keep my camera in the car with me most of the time, always trying to be ready for a photo opportunity. So the Wokingham Road a mile or so outside Reading was where I stopped to get the photo. I tried a few shots and ending up attaching my tele-conversion lens to zoom in on the scene. I had to use my car roof as a makeshift tripod and also had to contend with fading light. The picture really came into its own in editing. I used tinsii software which enabled me to convert the photo to black and white, and then reintroduce just the orange sunlight burst. I tweaked the brightness and contrast to give the photo a more ominous and dynamic feel, and finally I added a colour burst to the orange to breathe extra life into it. Sometimes it's the little things that can make all the difference to a photo. What appears to be a red kite flew into the shot as I pressed the shutter. This - added to the silhouetted tree and street light in the foreground - really makes the picture stand out.

3) Trees

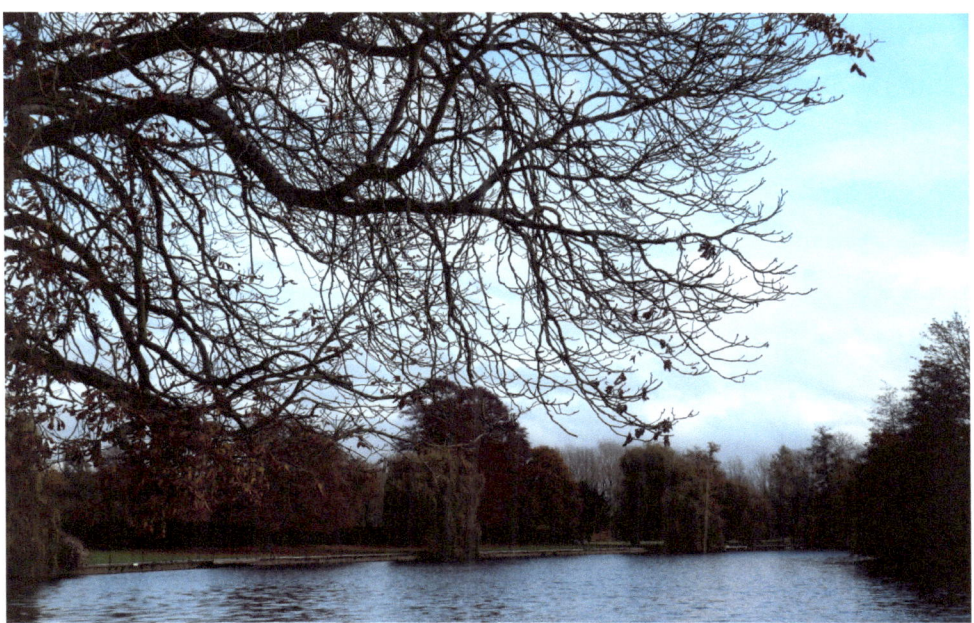

I spent 2 weeks totally fixated and obsessed with photographing trees and autumn is a great time of year for shooting them with the wonderful autumnal colours. The choice is wide open to shoot a entire tree, a tree set in a landscape, by dawn light, at night by the light of the moon, in colour, B&W or a silhouette! I drive many miles each week for work and this gave me the perfect opportunity to look at trees and to try and get the "perfect" tree. It soon became clear to me that trees in their own right are difficult subjects to photograph, so location, the possibility of having something else in the picture to add effect to the tree, and the time of day all became things to consider. I took numerous photos making it difficult to come down to a final choice, but in the end I went with my gut instinct and this picture shouted out at me straight away. The riverside location was on the Thames at Medmenham only a couple of minutes from work. This one pretty much came down to the beautiful location, and apart from a small crop to delete a piece of the riverbank in the foreground and a slight tweak to the contrast, this photo is exactly what you get.

I was pleased with the way the tree in the forefront creates a spider's web frame hopefully drawing the viewer to it, and hopefully it also draws the viewer across from the left to the right. The river isn't too overstated and then there is the background of wonderful trees in varying sizes and colours. Hopefully there is plenty to see! Photographing trees was a much tougher challenge than I thought it would be, but it really made me start to think about what I am photographing and the endless opportunities associated with every picture.

4) Christmas in Henley

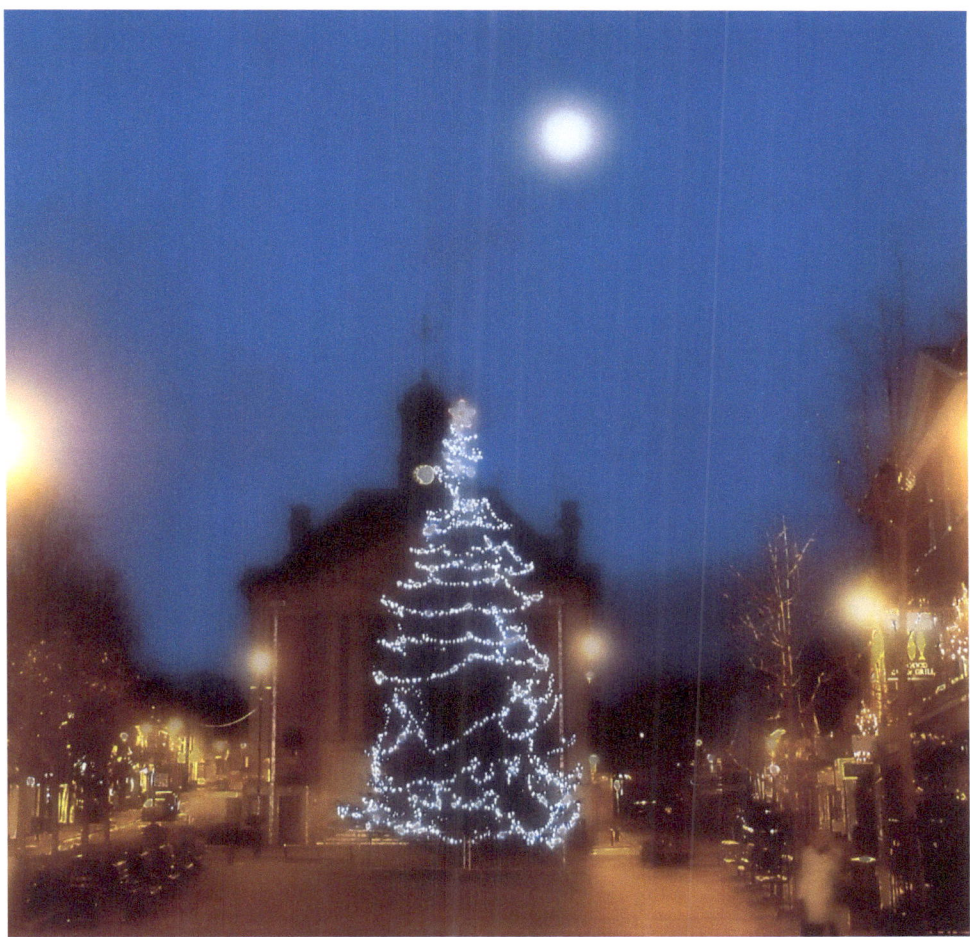

Trying to take a photograph to capture "Christmas" proved to be a bit more challenging than I thought it would be. Having had a lot of snow the previous two years leading up to Christmas, 2011 reverted back to the traditional snowless Christmas in the Thames Valley. So this was a little disappointing in scenic photographic terms as the selected photo would have been wonderful with a sprinkling of snow in it.

I took the picture in Henley on Thames at 7:30 in the morning to maximise the effect of the Christmas lights in between total darkness and the sun coming up. I was fortunate in that I was able to plan this photo as I drive past the square every morning on my way into work. Once the idea had occurred to me it was a case of waiting for a clear morning. I was very pleased that the moon played ball and took its place in the picture too! I played around with the brightness and contrast a bit, and decided in the absence of any snow to use a soft focus in the editing.

I think for me the picture captures a typical town centre Christmas scene at this time of the year, and I deliberately kept the street lights in the picture as it all adds to the festive atmosphere. There is a sense of timelessness about the scene, and the fact you can see someone shopping but not their detail. The viewer's eye takes in the tree as the main focal point as it should be, but then takes in the buildings, the person, the moon and the colours of the sky.

5) Rowers in Action

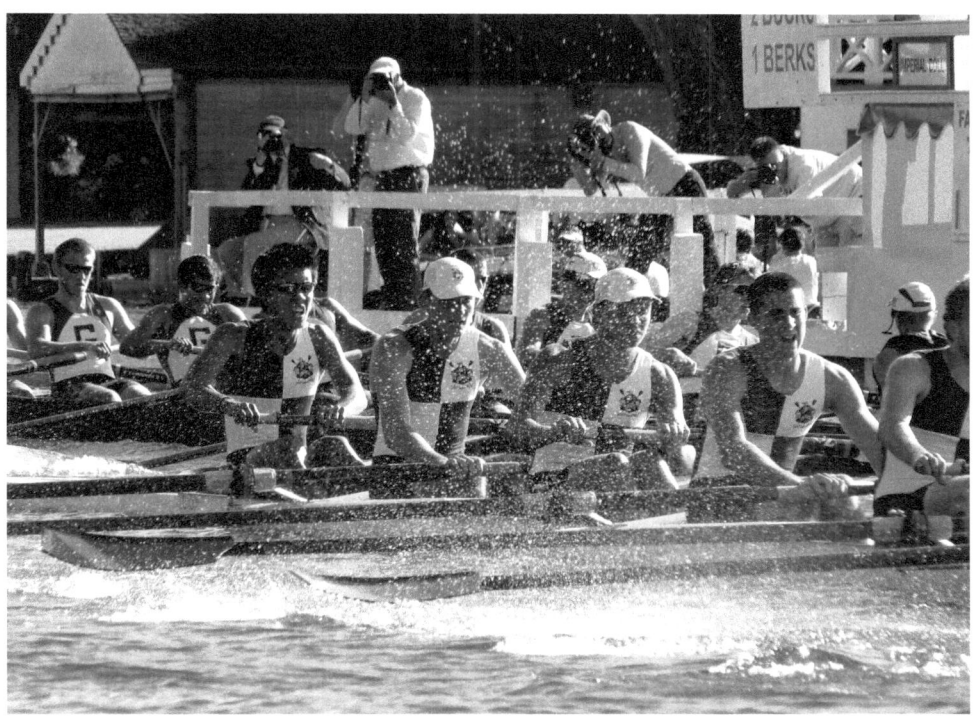

I soon discovered that pointing the camera at a random sporting activity was unlikely to achieve anything more than an average picture to be filed away in a photo album. My own sporting background is mainly football and cricket, but I also have a great affection for rowing as it was the sport of my late father. He was a keen local oarsman and represented Maidenhead Rowing Club at Henley Royal Regatta in the 1950s. On a rare hot summer's sunny day in 2012 I spent a lovely afternoon at Henley watching the rowing. The regatta dates back to 1839 and has some wonderful traditions. Gentlemen may not remove their jackets in the Stewards' Enclosure, which in hot summer temperatures cam make for a very hot day indeed. Ladies must wear dresses that cover the knee. Drinks may only be consumed in the designated bars and the use of mobile phones is prohibited anywhere in the enclosure. There are a number of areas along the river on the Berkshire side where the rowing can be viewed by the general public, and sometimes it is forgotten how popular the event is with the local community and is not just an event on the social calendar for "toffs" and corporate business.

There is no doubt that the social position of the event means that some in the Stewards' Enclosure (and elsewhere along the course) may have no interest in the actual rowing. I was fortunate enough to have a ticket for the enclosure so I relaxed in a deckchair snapping away by the Thames. The first problem I found when it came to taking a photo of the rowing was there were not too many close races and I wanted to get the idea of a race over in the photo. I set the camera mode to sports action and then spent a frustrating time never quite capturing the shot I wanted. So I tried a different approach, which was to change the camera setting to burst mode, used my knee as a makeshift tripod and when crews went by I just kept the shutter pressed. Finally I got a close race when Gonzaga College High School USA and Tabor Academy USA battled it out to the finish line, and I managed to get a photo that got everything I hoped I might get. The spray from the oars gives the photo motion and action. The effort on the two crews' faces shows just how much energy they put into the races. I think that taking the picture once the crews had passed - allowing the viewer to see their faces - means I got a better shot than the journalistic photographers did in the background of my shot. I turned the image to greyscale and then adjusted the brightness and contrast to give it a more documentary-type feel. I was very pleased with the end result.

6) Footwear

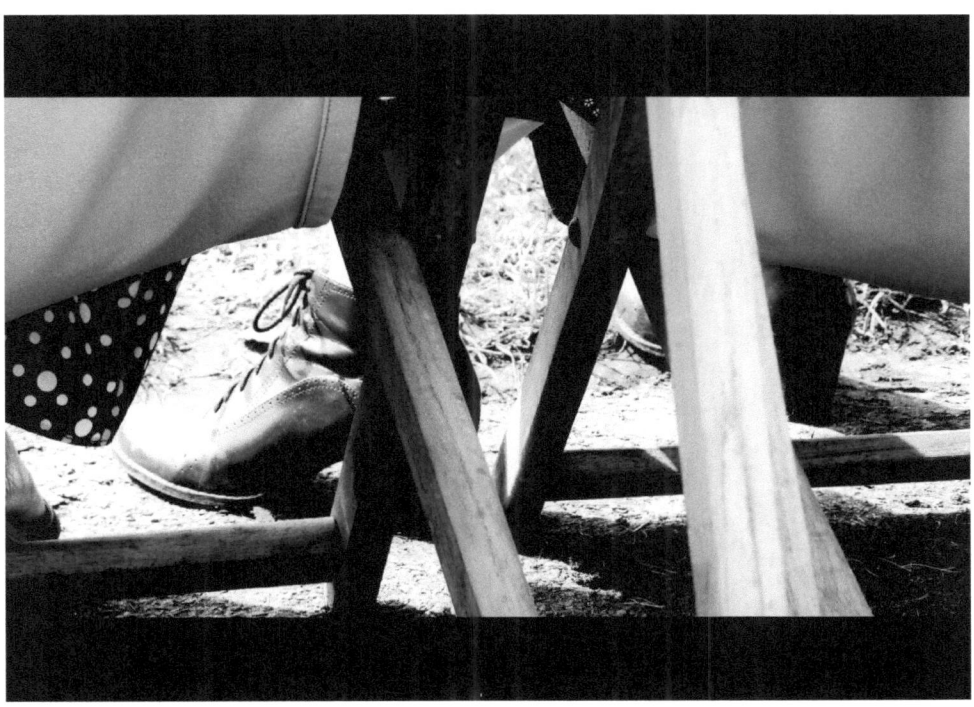

Sometimes it can be interesting to take a picture focusing in on something - be it a person, an object or a building for example. Sometimes taking pictures of a whole scene can end up taking something away from a potentially interesting photo. The purpose of this photo was to break the photographic Rule of Thirds that basically encourages you to set up your shot to be the most visually pleasing and dynamic as possible. The idea is that the eye of the viewer is led gently around the photograph and the various components within, and is not challenged by competing elements. I was thinking of going with a photo that would concentrate on the theme, rather than a picture of greater substance composition. Initially I experimented with photographing electricity pylons and paths through corn fields. These photos were successful, but they lacked a certain something and so I wanted to bring something more to the table.

It was whilst sitting in the deckchairs at Henley Royal Regatta that my creative juices kicked into action. I had spotted a pair of fabulous leather shoes in the row of chairs in front of me. The idea was to get the feet central in the shot and to completely disregard as much as possible all the usual rules of thirds grid lines. I used some quite dynamic editing to really get the best out of the photo. I used a black and white effect with tweaks to the brightness and contrast, and then used a cinematic effect to really capture the dramatic feel to the shot. I am always intrigued by people I don't know who appear in my photographs. We all lead such varied and fascinating lives, and I suppose I always like to bring an element of people watching into my photographs when the opportunity presents itself. By concentrating on just the shoes the idea is that the viewer will want to know more about the girl in the shoes.

7) The Sea at Prestatyn

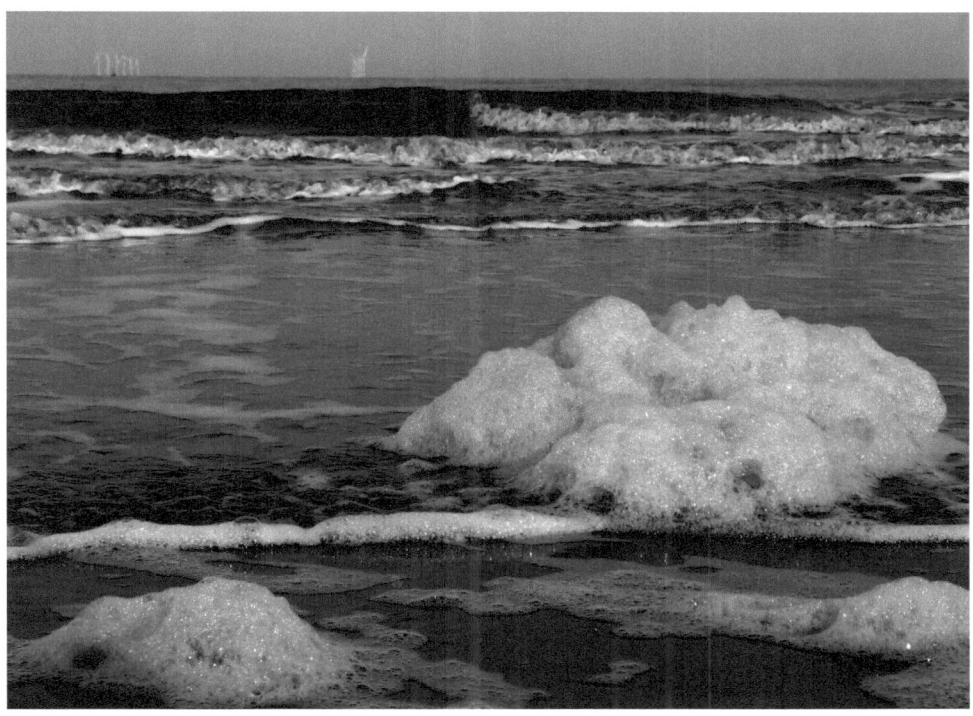

I love being close to water whether it be streams, rivers or the sea, and I could never tire of photographing water. I always feel calm and peaceful whenever I am close to water, although I am not sure where this comes from. I suspect my late father has played a role in this for as a young child I would enjoy my weekly trip to Maidenhead Rowing Club, where my father and his rowing club friends would meet on Sunday lunchtimes for drinks. It was not unknown for me to be allowed to finish the remains of his pint of beer! It is in fact a regret that I did nothing more than dabble with rowing as a teenager, and when I last rowed on the Thames one summer when I was in my early thirties I realised just what an opportunity I had let slip by.

When it came to photographing water as a subject I was lucky enough to have the opportunity to spend some time on the North Welsh coast. The photo was taken on the beach at Prestatyn in on a winter's morning in January. I had started by taking some photos using my tripod, and these were fine when I was taking a more landscape-style shot with the coastline in the background. I was fortunate to be there as the tide was turning and I was captivated by the almost bubble bath effect. The only way to get a decent shot of this was by lying down on the beach with the camera taking photos at ground level. I was especially pleased with this photo as not only is there interest at the forefront with the sea but the eye is also drawn to the wind farms on the horizon. I decided to go with black and white as I felt it gave a darker more powerful feel to the sea. I changed the brightness and contrast too to add to this effect.

8) Stonehenge

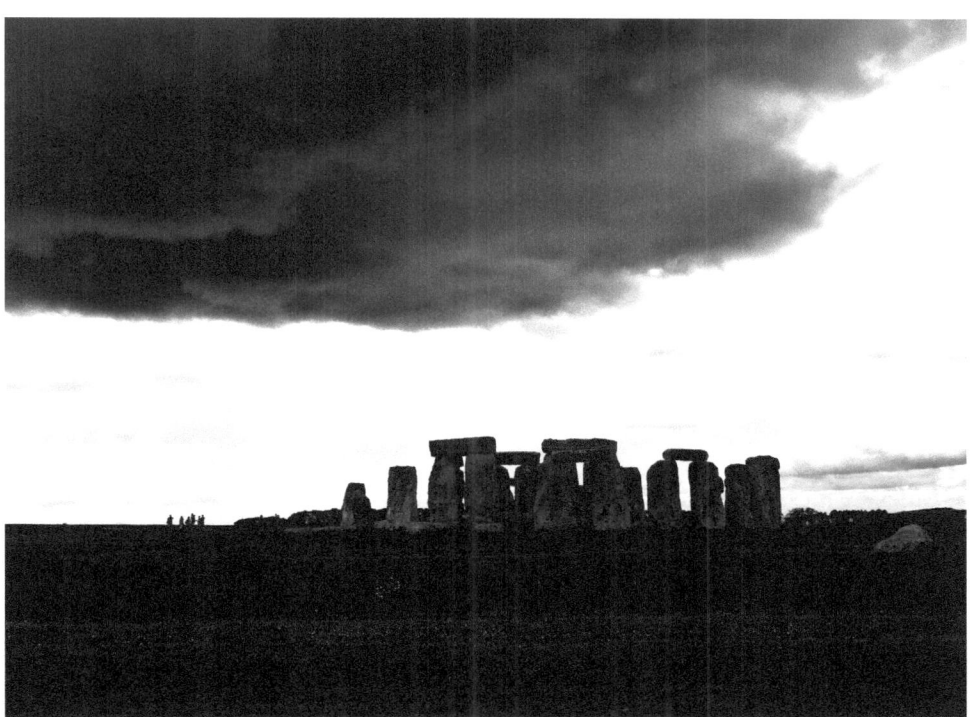

I have passed by the Stonehenge many times on my travels. There was a time with work when I would regularly drive back from Warminster to Marlow using the A344 to the A303 which would take me right past the stones, but I have never actually stopped and done the walking tour around it. In July my visiting Australian friends invited me to visit Stonehenge with them, and I jumped at the opportunity to play being a tourist for the afternoon. It was absolutely stunning and every angle gave you a slightly different view and perspective. The weather was all over the place with bright sunshine, threatening skies and heavy showers around and about, which made for some great sky backdrops. When I turned the photo into black and white it took on more of a silhouette feel to it reminding me a little of the album cover of The Joshua Tree by U2.

I think I prefer to remain a little bit in the dark about the story of Stonehenge and keep the myths and legends alive. I like to think that I was treading on the same land that Merlin once stood on. For an iconic historical attraction standing in a vast expanse of the English countryside, the whole place just was so atmospheric and it was lovely to be drawn to it if only for a short while.

9) Sunrise at Medmenham

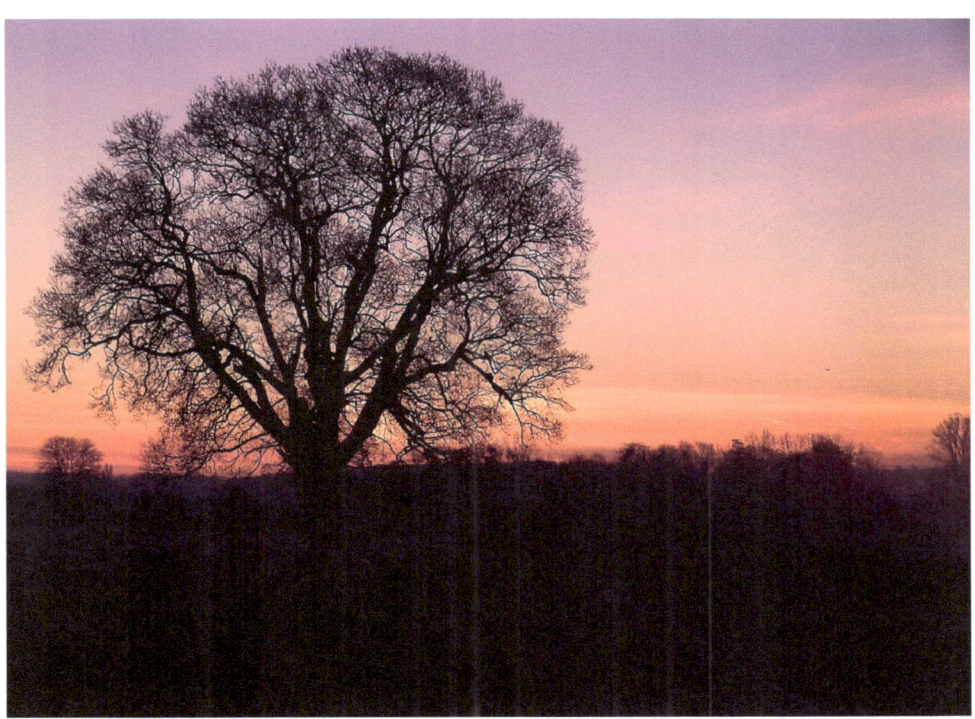

Driving into work each day means I get to see the seasons changing and how the local landscape changes with the seasons. For a few weeks over December and January I get to see the sunrise over Medmenham as I arrive at work. There is something inherently beautiful about winter landscapes and on this bitterly cold crisp morning in January 2012 I was able to capture the moment. The tree has also just about become my favourite tree, although I am not entirely sure why. Maybe it is because it stands alone aside the main road as I approach work so it looms up as I approach it every day, and I get to see it perfectly as it changes throughout the seasons. I love the way this tree in particular takes centre stage and yet the viewer by the very nature of the sunrise is also drawn to the trees in the background.

10) Canals and the Past

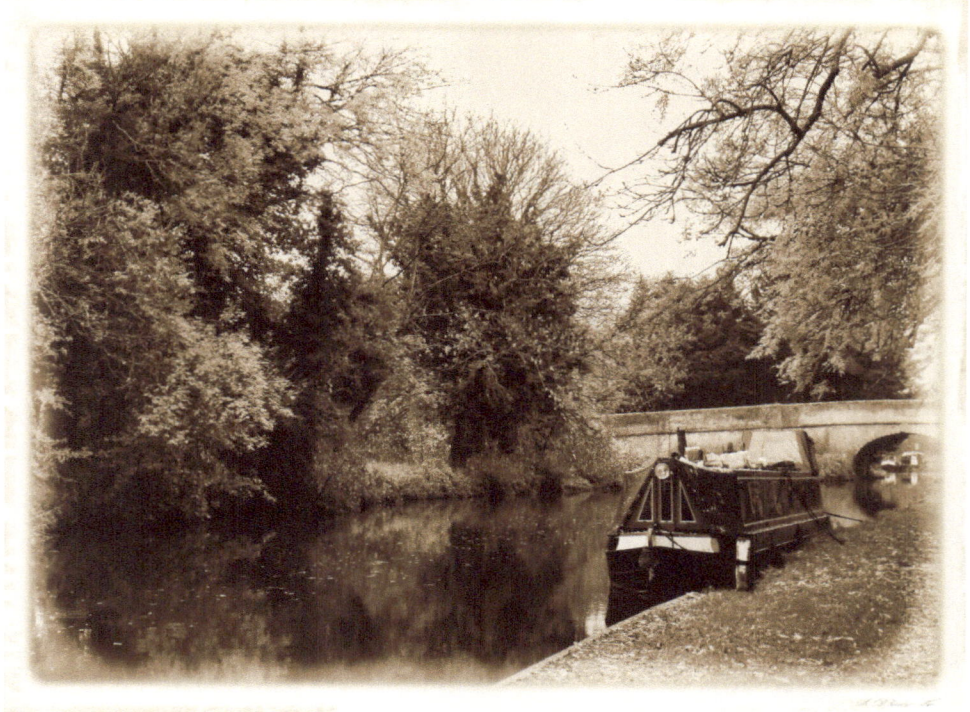

Sometimes when I watch historical dramas on television I am amazed at how they recreate such sets when all around us in the modern world the landscape is full of lights, cables, cars and of course the modern human being! I remember once driving into the village of Hambleden outside Henley whilst they were filming a period drama and was amazed at how they had transformed the village transporting it back in time.

The Kennet and Avon canal stretches 87 miles from the River Avon at Bristol to finally join the River Thames at Reading and the canal contains more than 100 locks. From Bristol to Bath the canal follows the path of the River Avon and from Newbury to Reading it links into the River Kennet. The canal dates back to the late 18th / early 19th century, but eventually fell into decline when the Great Western Railway opened in 1841. In the early 20th century the canal fell into disuse, but was reopened in 1990 following much restoration work.

The photo is taken along the stretch of the River Kennet at Burghfield just outside Reading, and it shows Burghfield Bridge. The river crossing in the area can be dated back to the 13th century. Just by the bridge is The Cunning Man pub, which is why I was there with my camera. Walking down the footpath with the old canal boats moored along the riverbank it occurred to me just how little would have changed in this setting over the last 100 years. Every sign of modern day life was missing, and I found this quite refreshing.

Modern day photo editing software allowed me to achieve the dated look. After converting the photo into black and white I used a "time machine" editing effect to recreate the Albumen photographic method widely used during the second half of the 19th century.

11) The Humber Bridge

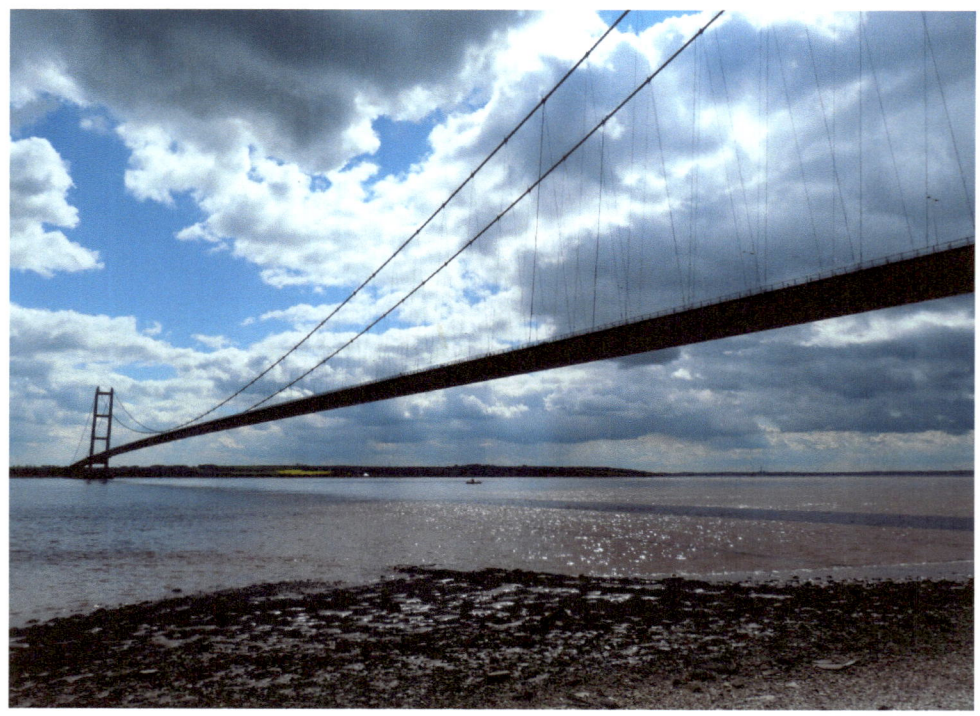

Photographing the Humber Bridge presented me with an immediate problem, the fact that it is miles from home. When the opportunity arose to take a work delivery up to Hull on a Saturday, I seized the chance to take in the Humber Bridge on my way home.

The Humber Bridge is a single span suspension bridge which opened in 1981 and which connects the East Riding of Yorkshire with North Lincolnshire. I first saw the bridge in 1985 when one of my best friends went to Hull University. Hull was the setting for quite a few mad weekends away. My memories of the city include the lack of bends in the roads with many of the streets appearing dead straight. Back in those days some of us would be partial to drinking Vodka and Orange chasers, and we were horrified when in Hull the orange was served as squash and not juice! Not long after my friend completed his degree, our family business picked up a new customer just outside Hull, and so I make the trip a couple of times a year.

This was my first opportunity to actually drive to the bridge itself and spend some time photographing it, and one thing I learnt is that sometimes photographs can require a lot of planning. Being so far from home my window of opportunity was small as I could only spend about an hour taking photos. I was therefore in the lap of the gods as far as the weather goes, and I was stuck with having to take a photo mid-afternoon whereas the lighting conditions at daybreak or sunset would have been better. Another problem was I wasn't really able to explore the local area to find the best places to take photos from, and so with hindsight it would probably have been easier to have stuck to a bridge closer to home and been able to really put more planning into the shot. So this was a big challenge, and in the short time I was there I got onto the bridge and onto the shoreline under the bridge too. For my chosen shot I was down on the beach by the bridge, and the sun came out for a few minutes and created a lovely shimmering effect on the water. Rather than zoom in on just the bridge I liked the "complete" effect I got with the photo: the beach in the forefront, the tiny boat under the bridge, the light reflection on the water and the wonderful backdrop of clouds. I would love to have another crack at this bridge as it is an amazing structure with endless photographic potential.

12) The Birthday Girl

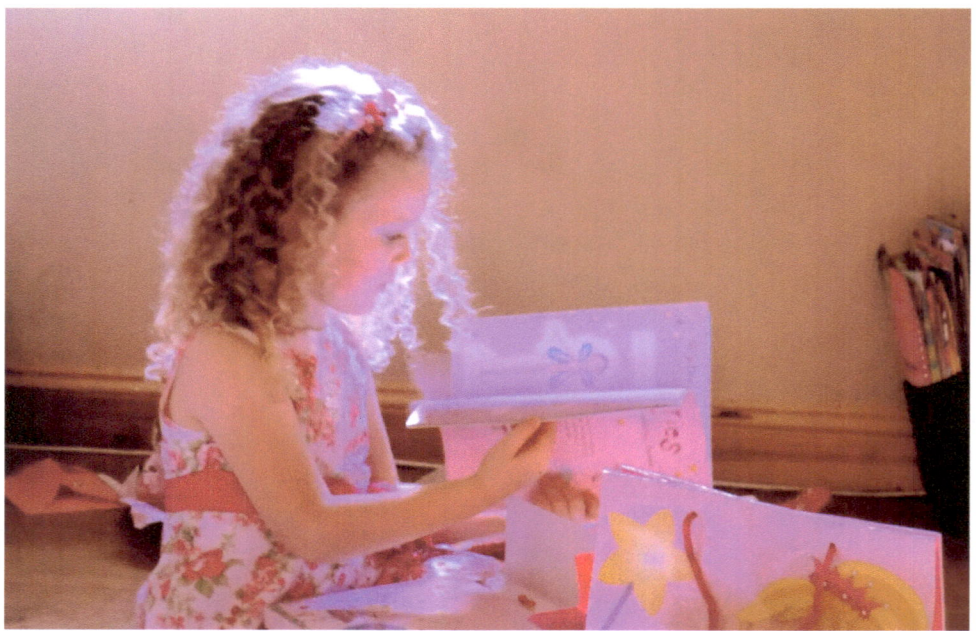

This photograph of my niece Anna was taken on her 5th birthday in September 2011. Photographing children can be difficult especially when they are aware of the camera being on them, and so sometimes the best photographs are the ones taken like this with they are completely unaware of the picture being taken. I think to be fair this can also be applied at times to photographing adults.

Technically this photo is not one of the best photos I have ever taken, as it was taken on my compact camera and it really was more about capturing a special moment in time. The sunlight cast a lovely glow around Anna highlighting her gorgeous curls and she was enthralled with her presents and cards.

13) War Memorial

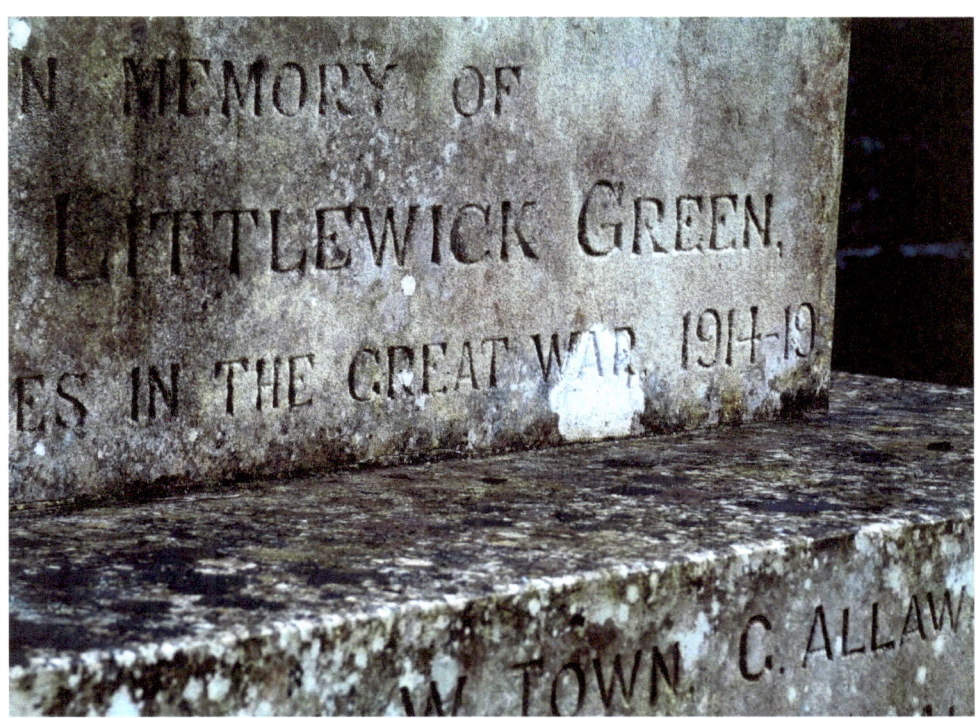

In many churches the length and breadth of the land war memorials are found. This memorial is set in the churchyard of the church of St. John the Evangelist in the village of Littlewick Green in Berkshire. Littlewick Green plays a big part in my parents' history. As a parish it is where my mother and father got married and lived before they built their house in Maidenhead. My grandparents on my mother's side ran The Coach and Horses pub for 30 years or so. People familiar with the area will now know this place as The Shire Horse. Not only did my mother live in a pub in the parish, but she was actually born at The Sun Inn pub in Henley! Mum's keen connection with horses meant that whilst we children were growing up she was secretary of the horse show section of Littlewick Show. When my father sadly passed away in 2009 my mother's greatest wish was that he could be laid to rest in the churchyard, which she was granted, therefore cementing our family's connection with parish.

War memorials can be beautiful pieces of work, whilst at the same time reminding those of us fortunate enough never to have had to serve our country the great sacrifice that so many people have made during the two world wars and continue to do to this very day. I have always been interested in history and find the black and white footage of the two world wars fascinating. My grandfather on my father's side fought in the First World War and as a young child I was fascinated by scars on a leg wound he got. It was however the gas attacks that were to affect his health in a more lasting way. When I took the photo I was surprised to see the date showing 1914-19 when the war ended in 1918. I learned that although armistice was declared on 11th hour of the 11th day of the 11th month in 1918, the peace treaty was not signed in Versailles until the 28th of June 1919.

I decided to go for a close-in shot of the memorial. As beautiful as the memorial is, I thought as well as the interesting date inscription, a partial reveal of the names of soldiers brings a touch of emotion and the sheer significance of what it stands for. The main thing that I had to do in editing was to use heavy contrast to bring out the engraved lettering. I think this photograph is one of the more emotionally significant shots I have taken.

14) Wembley Stadium

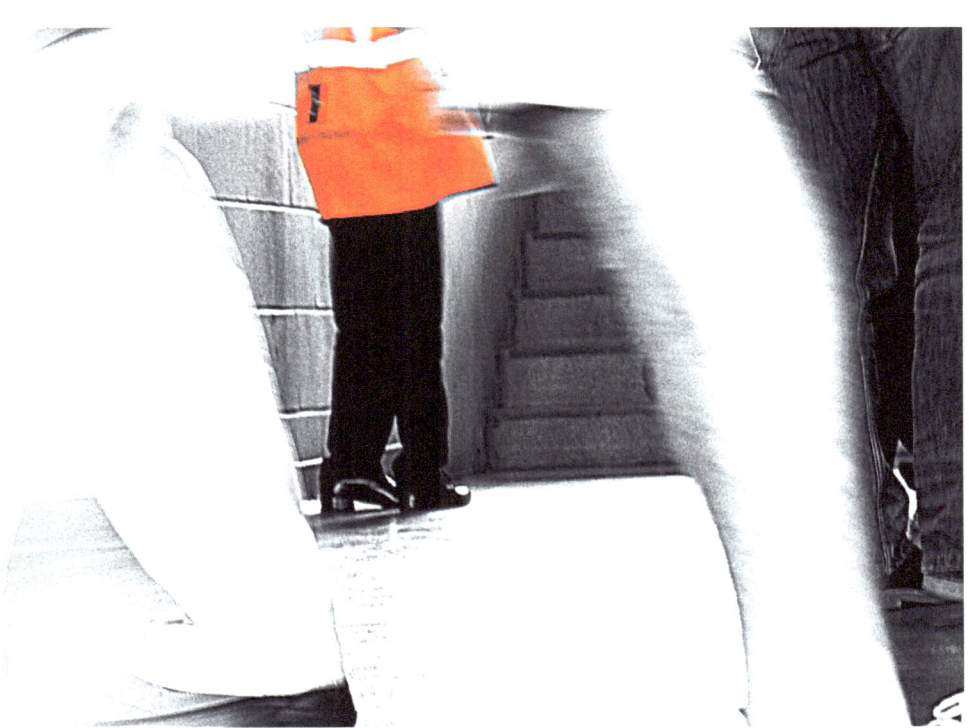

This photograph was taken at the new Wembley Stadium on 3rd of August during the London Olympics of 2012 at the Mexico versus Senegal quarter-final match, which Mexico won 4-2 after extra time. My story with Wembley however starts almost 40 years earlier on 24th January 1973 when my father took my brother and me to Wembley to see the World Cup qualifier between England and Wales. I was a few weeks short of my 8th birthday, and it was a school night so what an adventure for two young boys. The game was a 1-1 draw with John Toshack giving the Welsh the lead, but Norman Hunter scoring a spectacular long range equaliser for England. We stood right up behind the goal opposite the tunnel and it was my first ever professional match. I can clearly remember telling people at school the next day about it and not even my teacher believed me.

Over the subsequent years I have been to some memorial football matches and music concerts there. I was fortunate enough to see Arsenal win an FA Cup Final replay against Sheffield Wednesday back in 1993 with a goal scored in the last minute of extra time. I was also very lucky to see all England's games in EURO 96 at Wembley, an experience I will never forget. My musical history there was always somewhat hindered by me drinking too much. I saw U2 there on The Joshua Tree tour and wasn't really sure where the stage was by the time they came to play. Worse was to follow when I went to see Bryan Adams as I spent the whole of his set drinking at the bar and then managed to miss the last bus home meaning I spent the night sleeping on a bench outside under the stars at Hammersmith Broadway. The building of the new Wembley has so far led to perfect behaviour at a U2 concert on the 360 tour, and at the Olympic football.

The idea behind the photo was to try taking photos at a low angle to photograph things from a different perspective. It was somehow fitting that I was back at Wembley taking photos from closer to the height I was back at my first visit in 1973. The photo was taken on the concourse during half-time, when people were getting their half-time refreshments. I decided to focus the camera on a steward in an orange jacket, and therefore as people walked past I was able to get a sense of motion into the photo. In editing I turned the photo into black and white and just reintroduced the colour into the orange jacket and I feel there is great contrast between the person walking right in front of the camera in the foreground and the bright jacket in the background.

15) The Eiffel Tower

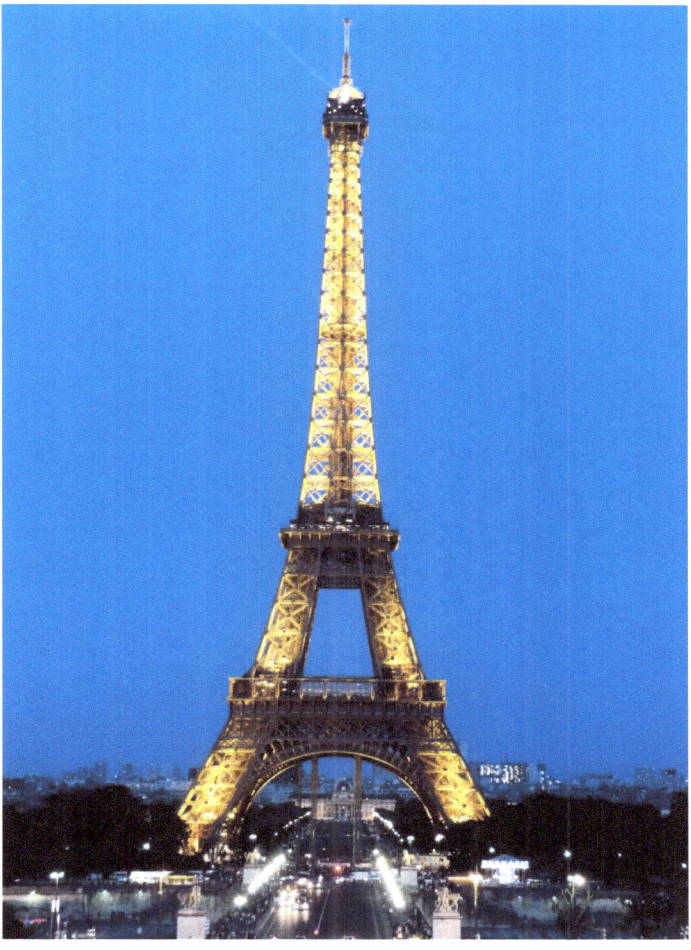

My visits to France have been very few and far between in my lifetime. I played football in Metz close to the German border for Maidenhead Boys in 1978. I enjoyed a boozy birthday in Calais in my late twenties and spent a break at Euro Disney in my thirties. It was on that trip that I spent a day sightseeing around Paris and that had been my only experience until the summer of 2012 when I spent a wonderful 24 hours in the city with my amazing Australian friends.

The trip was pretty much a last-minute idea and I got the Euro Star from Kings Cross / St. Pancras on a Saturday morning, arriving in Paris late afternoon to meet up with my friends. We enjoyed a lovely meal along the Champs-Elysées with the Arc de Triomphe providing a spectacular backdrop. We then travelled on a tour bus to the Eiffel Tower as the sun was setting and night was drawing in, which gave the perfect conditions to photograph this magnificent structure. I tried various exposure settings to try and get the best photo possible and eventually settled on this photo which was taken just after the sun had set and the tower's illuminations had been turned on. It really was the most beautiful sight. There was nothing to do in editing and this photo is exactly how it was taken.

The weekend was finished as on the Sunday the Tour de France reached its conclusion in Paris and my friends had booked us fantastic seats near the finish line. This was even luckier for me as it meant I got see Bradley Wiggins become the first Englishman to win the race in its 99-year history. In the morning before the race my friend Andrew had booked a once-in-a-lifetime treat and joined a group of fellow Australians who got to cycle twice around the circuit running along the Champs-Elysées. As the race drew closer the atmosphere continued to build and the whole spectacle was just fantastic. During those wonderful 24 hours I fell in love with Paris, and it is a place I am keen to return to and get to know a whole lot better.

16) Sunset on the M4 Motorway

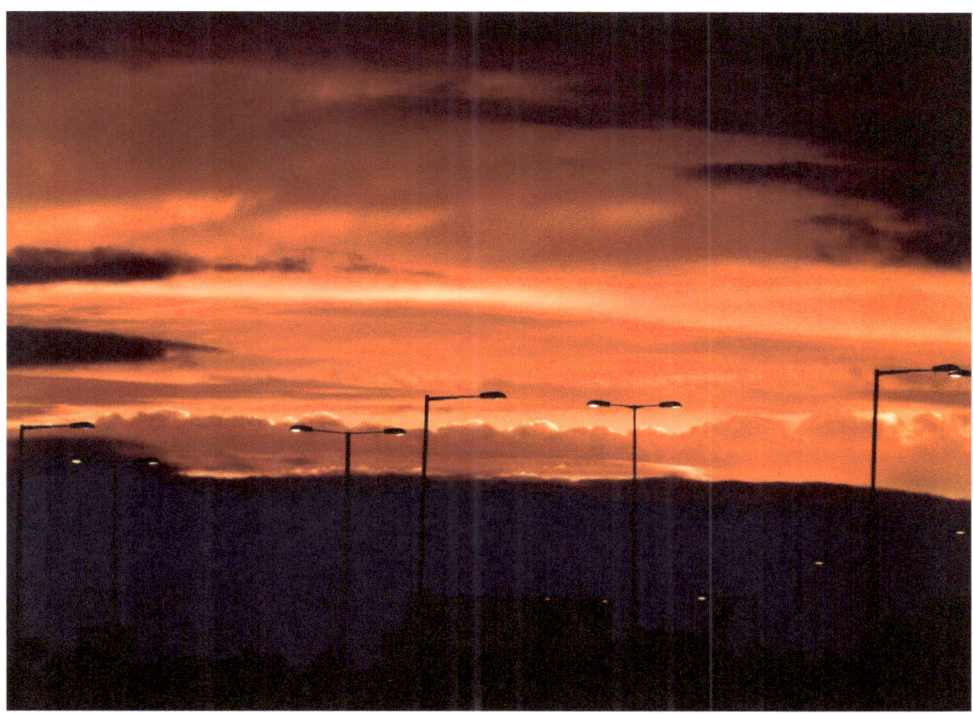

Sometimes the most unlikely settings can provide great locations for photography. I have come to the conclusion that a beautiful sunset can provide the perfect backdrop to pretty much any location. I can remember the M4 motorway when its eastern end terminated at Maidenhead. As a child I would be very excited when we travelled on the motorway and would enjoy spotting the landmarks as I headed into London with my parents. My classic mistake was mistakingly reading "Cold Snacks" as "Cold Snakes" at the Heston Services! Snakes are probably my most hated creature on the planet! My dad would also tell us how far the guns on HMS Belfast could project missiles. He would point to a bridge on the M4 using it to show the distance missiles could in theory travel from its mooring by Tower Bridge, and I always felt slightly relieved once we had passed that point.

The setting for the photo was the section near Junction 6 at Slough, and the photo was taken from the A332 close to the Eton College playing fields as I looked across to the motorway and the amazing sunset. This was another of those completely unplanned photos. I was driving home from Datchet and it was one of those long summer evenings with a glorious sun setting. At first I could only see the beautiful red skyline and I was wondering where I could stop to photograph as fortunately I had my camera with me. I thought that somewhere in Eton would be perfect, but viewpoints looking westwards didn't present themselves, and I knew that once I got back onto the motorway the opportunity would be lost. In the end I pulled over on the roadside verge and started to think what I could do as I wasn't sure that looking over towards the motorway and Slough would provide a very good backdrop. I was mistaken as the picture captures the beautiful sunset and I also think has an interesting foreground to keep the viewer interested. It is a picture literally on two contrasting sections, the top half showing the beautiful setting, and then the articulated lorry heading west along the motorway towards what look like pretty ominous clouds moving in.

The challenge I had in editing was how to bring both sections out in the photo. In the end I made two copies of the same photo and then merged them together. In one photo I concentrated on bringing out the colours of the sunset, and in the other photo I concentrated on making the lorry and motorway visible, and having done that I used software to bring the two copies together as one photo. I really like this photo as it is a little unusual, and has plenty going on to draw in the viewer.

17) Ship in a Bottle

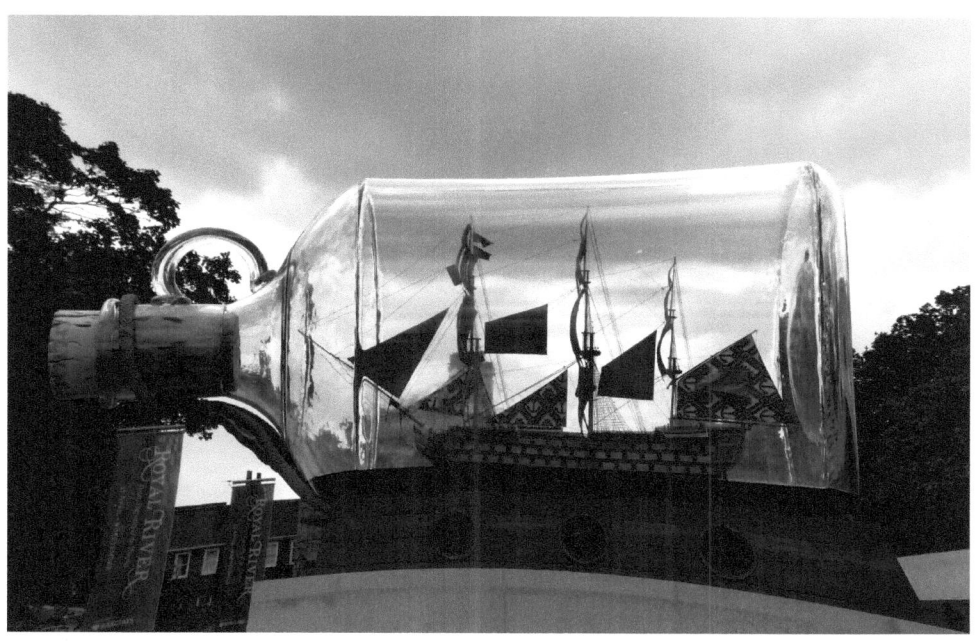

Greenwich was the setting for the ship in a bottle photograph. I spent a very enjoyable afternoon wandering around Greenwich a month or so before the London 2012 Olympics, and there was an excitement and an air of expectation around the place. In contrast to my only previous visit to Greenwich as an A-Level student in the early 1980s, when we spent an afternoon in the pub playing pool ignoring the culture and stunning views that Greenwich has to offer. However we all grow up some day, and to be fair I thoroughly enjoyed my afternoon playing pool and drinking beer.

I took in many of the main attractions including the Cutty Sark, the National Maritime Museum, the Royal Observatory and Sir Christopher Wren's Old Royal Naval College. I hadn't realised that there is also a foot tunnel underneath the Thames linking Greenwich with the Isle of Dogs. I captured all the landmark sights and the biggest decision was which photograph to put into this book from a choice of many. In fact when got there I was rather taken aback at the amount of photo opportunities that presented themselves one after another, and with hindsight I would liked to have stayed there a bit longer or maybe put in a little more planning before going. However it is not a difficult journey to make and I am sure will return there again sometime soon.

The photo that I have chosen is of Nelson's Ship in a Bottle, which is a recent addition to Greenwich outside the National Maritime Museum created by artist Yinka Shonibare. The miniature ship is a painstakingly crafted 1/30th replica of Nelson's HMS Victory, and it was on board this battleship Nelson died during the Battle of Trafalgar on October 21st 1805. Such is the attention to detail that the replica ship has 80 cannon and 27 sails set as on the day of battle. During editing I wanted to highlight the boat inside the bottle and give it greater presence on the photo, so I used tinsii software to remove some of the colours from the photo retaining just the boat in colour. For added effect I then used fish eye distortion to add extra panoramic effect to the photo.

18) Just an Eye

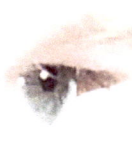

High key photography is a technique used to produce bright images using a high exposure setting on the camera. The image will normally be devoid of shadows, which is done by manipulation of exposures to overexpose the image thus removing shadows. The resulting images are generally calm and peaceful for the viewer. The picture is a self-portrait of my eye and it was set up in a bedroom with my white backdrop draped over the bed as I had no way of hanging it up. I set the camera up on a tripod and on the 10 second timer setting meaning I had to get around to the front and lie down on the floor on my stomach in order to get into shot. I also used a light reflector, which brought life into the eyes. I thought that I would have to use editing software to get the finished article, but actually I didn't tweak the picture at all in post-production. The only thing I did was to crop the original photo, so what you see in the photo is my eye against the white backdrop. I was really happy with this exposure as it is hard to make out the line of my forehead above the eye.

19)   Magnolia in Bloom

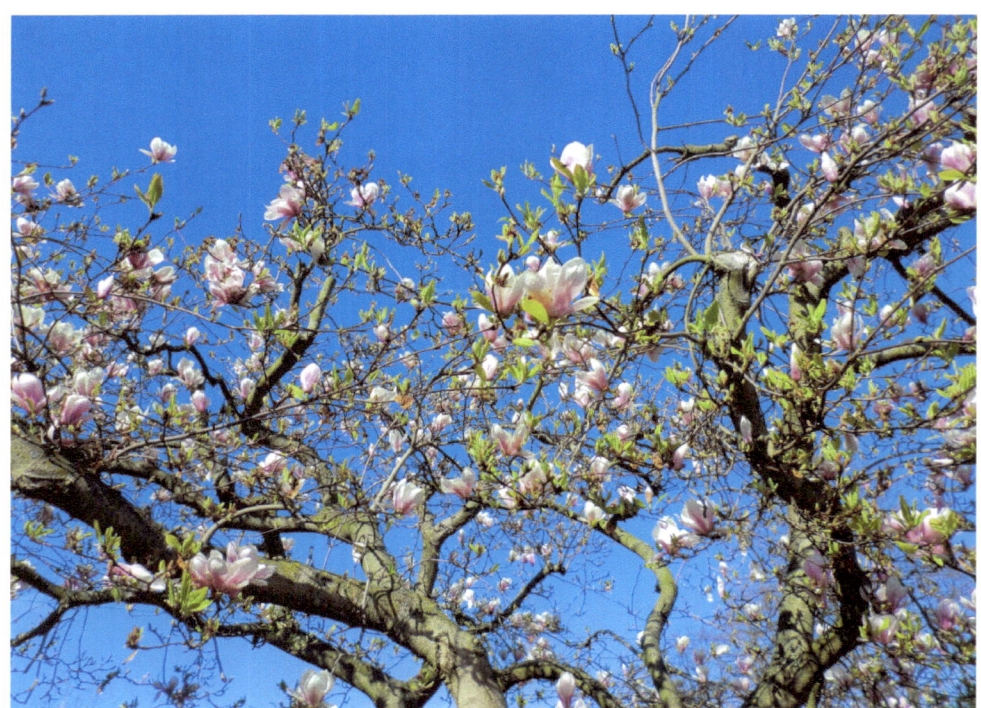

Springtime is one of my favourite times of the year, with longer lighter days, and the countryside coming to life. For me there is no better sight than a magnolia tree in full bloom, and this photo really was a spur of the moment effort with my compact camera one Sunday afternoon when I was walking into Maidenhead. The clear blue skies provided a perfect backdrop and after a few attempts I preferred this close-up shot rather than one of the whole tree. We have planted a couple of trees at my mother's house, one in the front garden and one in the back, but it will take many years for them to mature into something as wonderful as this one. The road where the tree is located is a road I have walked down throughout my whole life, and yet this was probably the first time I noticed the magnolia tree. I am not sure what that says about me, but I would like to think that even the most familiar surroundings can bring us new experiences.

20)   Lunch on the Slopes

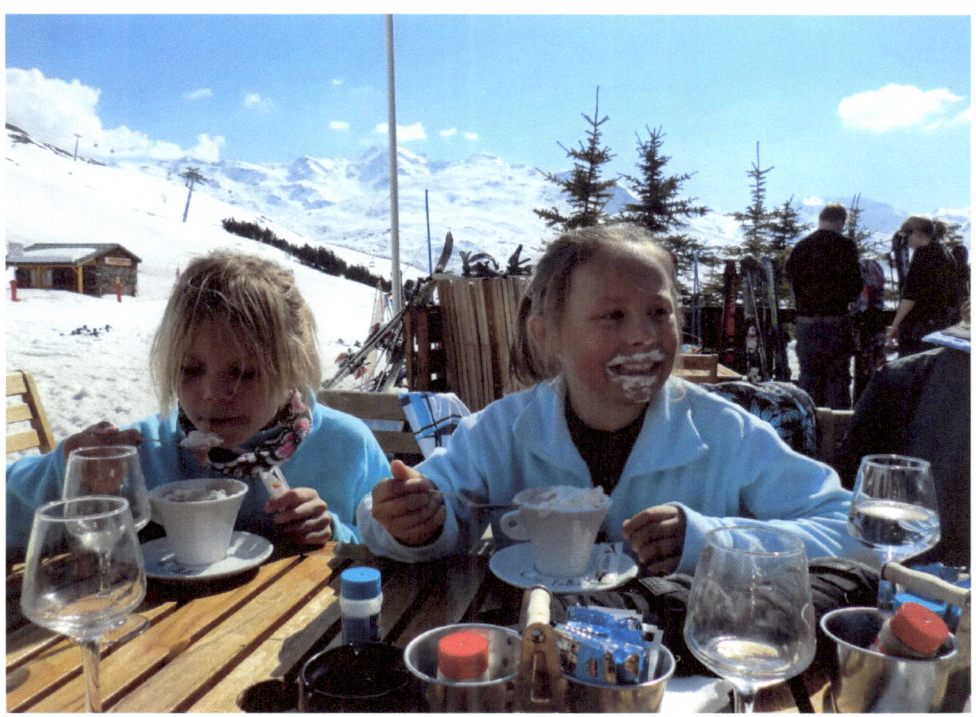

I am a pretty novice skier. I went on a school skiing trip to Austria in 1981 I think, and then on a two week holiday to Bulgaria in 1988. It was not until 2011 that I next went skiing, this time to Courchevel in the French Alps. I am fortunate enough to have good friends, the Maclean family, who have a chalet there. It has now become an annual event as I returned for a weekend skiing in 2012. I spent a good deal of time on my backside, but that did not diminish my enjoyment for one minute. I was very grateful to my friends who waited for me on countless occasions to pick myself up out of the snow. My friendship with Calum goes back over twenty years when he worked in Southampton with one of my old school friends, and many a good night was spent in the bars and clubs of Southampton. Calum and Mary Anne now have four children, one of whom stars in the photo, and a more welcoming and friendly family you could not wish to meet.

The idea was to try and take a spontaneous random photo capturing people in a moment in time, thereby hopefully drawing the viewer in. I had taken my compact camera with me on the slopes, and we had been blessed with the most fantastic sunny day, with hardly a cloud in the sky and far too hot for skiing. After a physical morning on the slopes we stopped for lunch at one of the lovely restaurants scattered on the various runs, and I took the opportunity to take this shot. My friend's daughter Emma had a hot chocolate topped with a mountain of cream and she wasted no time dunking her face into it. For me the picture captures the emotion of the moment, and to be fair of the whole weekend. This photo shows happiness, laughter and most of all fun. The scenic backdrop is great, although I think the face is the absolute focal point of this photo, and although I could have cropped the photo I decided to go with the whole scene, which I think captures everything.

21)   Nature on Your Doorstep

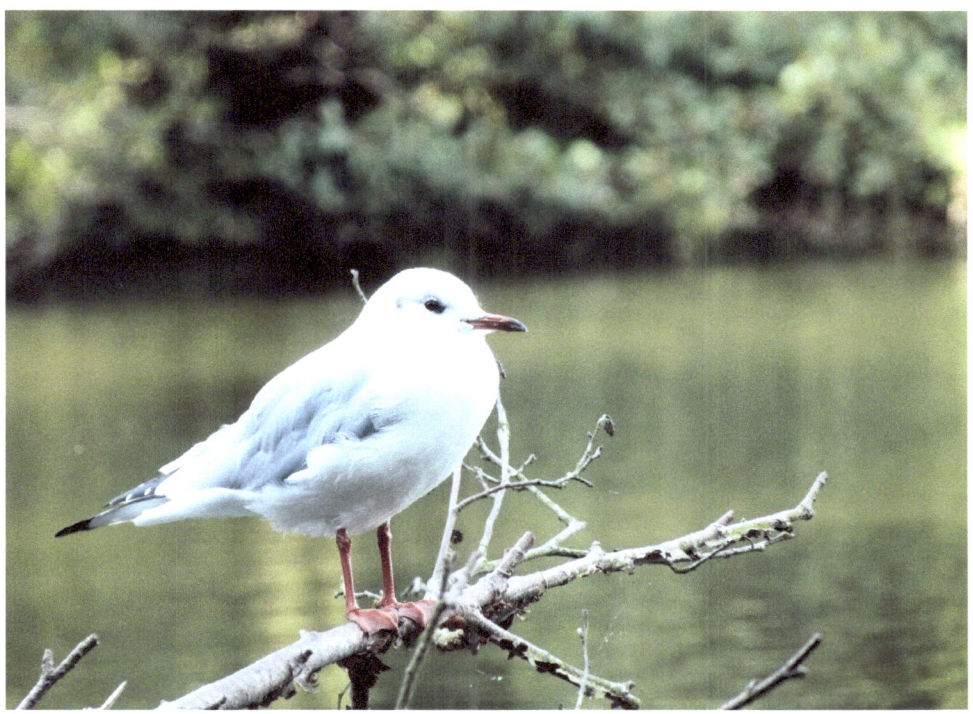

Just a few minutes' walk from my front door is the picturesque Whiteknights Lake. The lake, a designated conservation area, is now part of Reading University which took over the site in 1947. The lake is a beautiful and peaceful place and pretty much a hidden gem, as like many people I have always been aware of its existence without ever bothering to go in, something which I have now rectified.

I was not intending to photograph birds on this particular visit, as I was hoping to photograph some autumn colour. In fact I am not a keen or knowledgeable birdwatcher, but photographing birds can be extremely rewarding when you finally get that shot. I spotted this Black-headed Gull perched on a fallen branch and loved the way it seemed to enjoy a rather grandiose status watching over the other birdlife in the lake. I simply used the nature setting on my camera, which made for a close-up shot and the depth of field effect really sets the photo up perfectly.

22)   A Blast of Snow

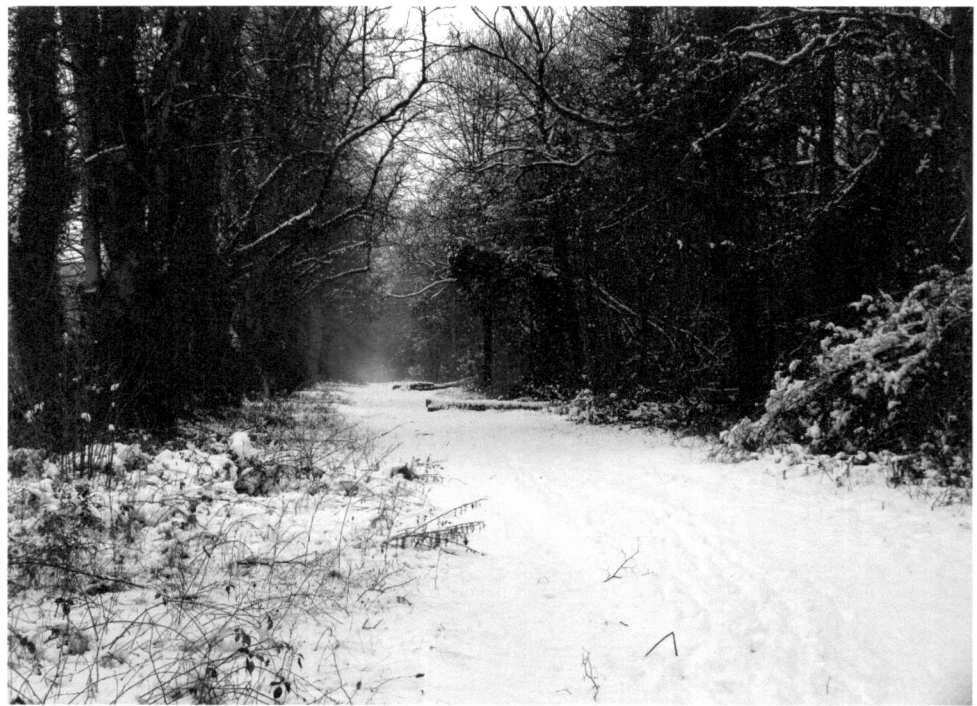

Maidenhead Thicket situated to the west of the town is the place where I spent much of my childhood. It is just a few minutes' walk from my parents' house and the place where mum grew up in the pub and riding horses. Times were different back then when I was a child. I spent so many days riding my bike exploring the thicket on my own, sometimes making up my own imaginary games and only returning home when it was feeding time. Of course these days in such a more dangerous world it would not be possible to allow a young child to go off for hours like I was able to do back then. Some of the pathways would lead to craters, which were caused by bombs falling on the thicket during the Second World War. This is not so surprising as the thicket is located very close to White Waltham Airfield which was home to the Air Transport Auxiliary during the war. Civilian pilots took over the duties of service pilots to fly newly-built aircraft from airfields such as White Waltham to Royal Air Force and Royal Navy military front line squadron airfields, and during the course of the war 309,000 were transported in such a manner.

Having had two pretty cold and miserable winters, the winter of 2011/12 was mercifully not as cold and we only had a couple of days of snow. In the south-east of England the first sign of snow means the whole road system is likely to grind down to gridlock in part due lack of road treatment and also in part to inexperienced drivers in such conditions.

The day I took this photo was one of the better snowy days. There had been enough snow to settle on the ground, but it was the wet snow that doesn't usually settle on the roads, which made driving easy. The picture was in fact taken right alongside the busy A4 running between Maidenhead and Reading. I pulled into a lay-by and only had to walk a few paces to get the shot. I turned the photo into black and white and tweaked the contrast as it brought out the beautiful snowy mist in the background, which was being caused by the wind gently blowing snow off the branches. I was really pleased with this effort, and also it shows that sometimes you can literally get a decent shot in any location.

23)   A Full Moon

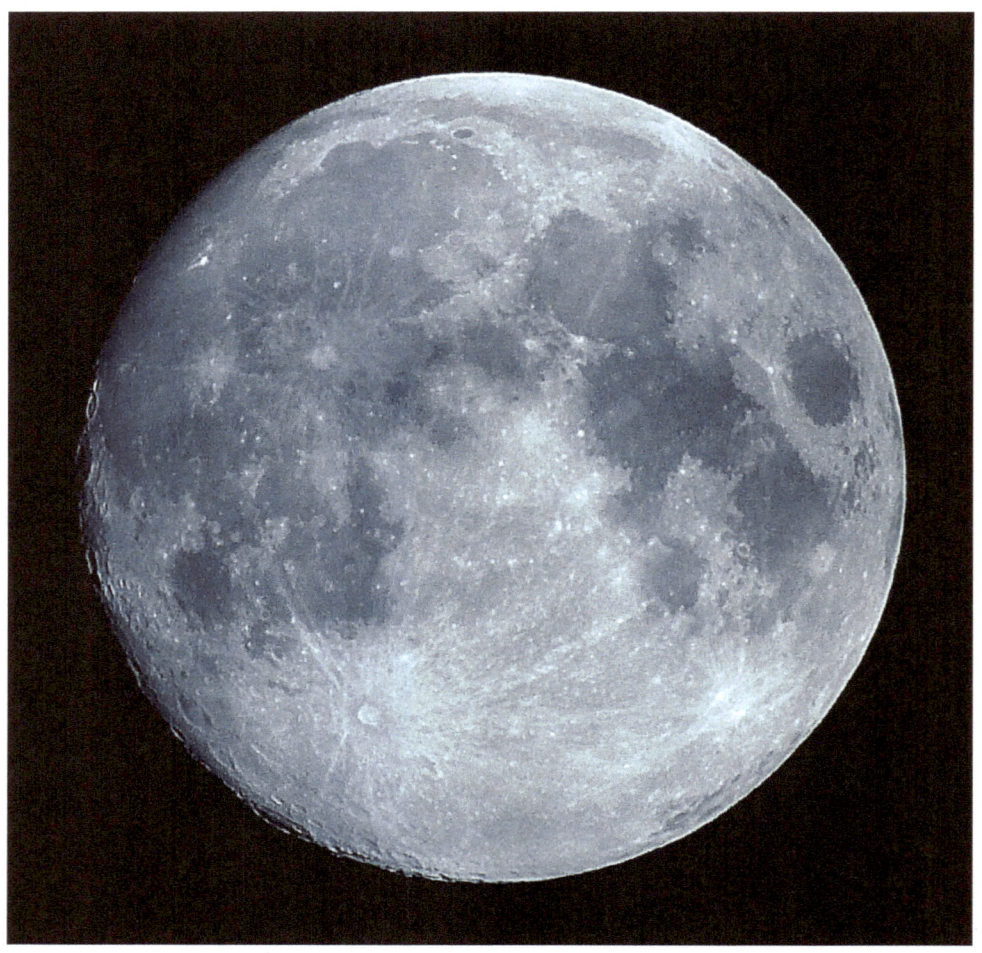

My first memory of the moon goes back to my first family holidays at Pagham, close to Bognor Regis on the south coast. I vaguely remember the family sitting around a tiny black and white television watching the Apollo landings on the moon, which may have even been the first lunar landing on July 20th 1969. We would spend a week there every summer in a bungalow right on the beach owned by relatives. We would play cricket test matches in the front garden, play on the beach, be allowed a bag of pennies to go down to the amusement arcade, and on one day during the week the big treat was a trip into Bognor to Hamleys toy shop.

I found photographing the moon fascinating as I really had to get to know my camera's functionality and capabilities in order to get the best shot possible. The moon itself presents so many different types of photographic opportunities such as time of day as it can appear during the day or night, although one of the best times of the day for photographing the moon is twilight, which helps pick out details in the surroundings and add interesting colours to the sky and clouds. My first attempts to photograph the moon just after I had got the camera were not successful. I made elementary mistakes such as holding the camera by hand and using the intelligent auto feature, so for this photo I planned in much more detail. Using my trusty tripod meant that there would be no camera shake giving me a much better chance to get a shot in focus. Although my Lumix FZ45 doesn't have an automatic shutter cable option, I was able to use the timer to make sure the camera was perfectly still when the shot was taken. For night photography keeping the camera still is absolutely vital. I attached my tele-conversion lens, which allowed me to get a good close-up shot. I read up and then experimented with shutter settings so as not to over- or underexpose the picture, and took the photo with an exposure setting of 1/60 second and an ISO setting of 100. The picture was taken 24 hours before the actual full moon. In editing I used a slight blue tint on the photo which added that final missing piece.

24)   A World of Books

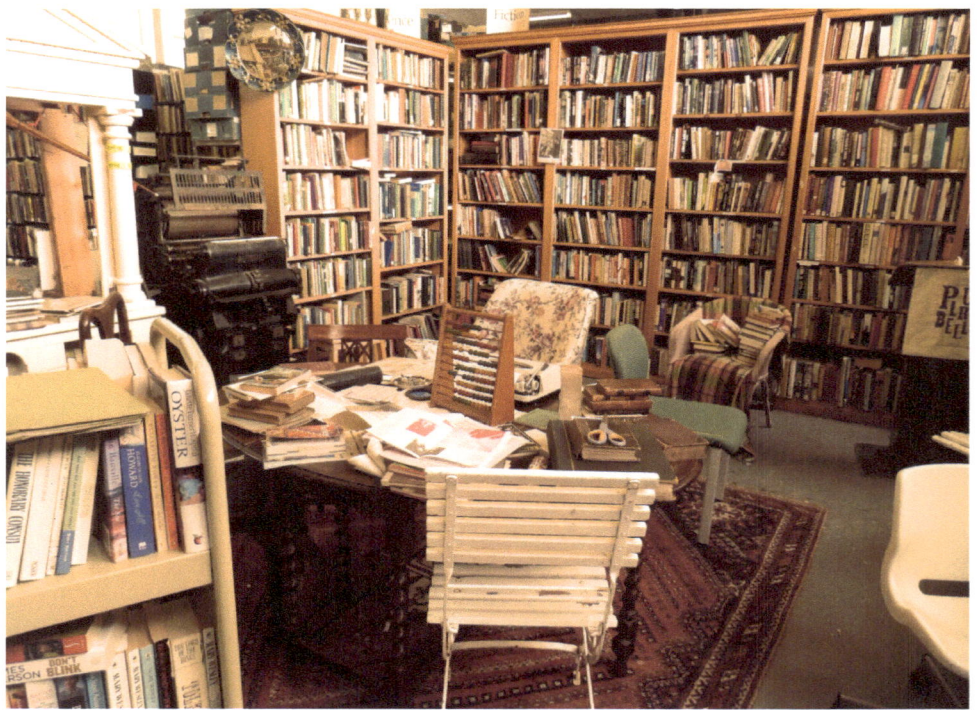

After 28 years in the family business my work still never ceases to surprise me. No two days are ever the same when it comes to selling packaging materials, but more interestingly I never know who the next customer is going to be. Over the years I have delivered into Windsor Castle, been suspected of being an IRA terrorist whilst delivering polythene sheeting close to the Old Bailey, supplied many prisons with property bags and even printed carrier bags for my favourite band The Alarm. 2012 brought a new gem of a customer called Plurabelle Books selling second hand books based in the heart of Cambridge. I spent a lovely hour there one Saturday morning delivering some goods on my way up to a wedding in Lincolnshire, and as soon as I entered it I felt as though I had been transported into another world. The business occupies an old stonemasons' workshop close to the railway station, and they very aptly describe their premises as an Aladdin's cave. The barn contains over 70,000 titles all of which are for sale, and many of the books cost only a pound or two.

The photo shows one corner of the building, and I love the way they have created a dated library-type atmosphere. It was quite a challenge to represent everything I saw in just one photo, but I think it gets across much of what I saw. I toyed with the idea of turning the photo into black and white or using a softer focus, but in the end I tweaked the brightness and contrast and added a tungsten lighting effect to warm up the picture. I was pleased with the end result and think it works really well. I feel it does get the photo pretty close to matching the daylight conditions I took the original photo in, or perhaps the conditions I imagine I took the photo in. I could not leave there without buying a book, and I discovered a wonderful old book of London, photographed in black and white, that contained some fantastic photos. One could be forgiven in an era of a world gone Kindle mad in thinking that the days of the good old-fashioned book might be numbered. Maybe places like this prove that there is still a massive demand for the traditional book, and I was one satisfied customer proving the point.

25)   Windsor Castle at Night

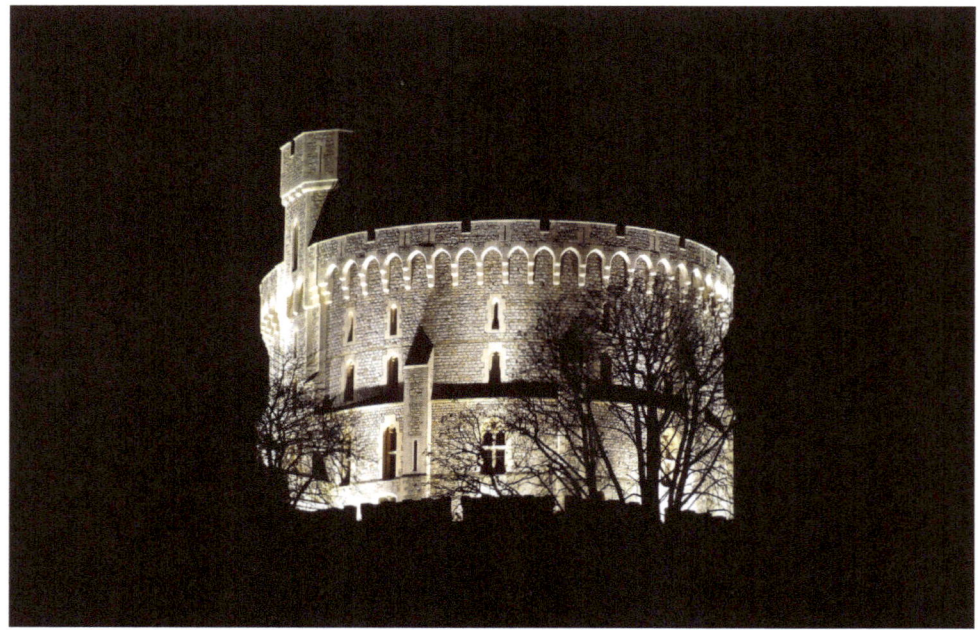

I have fond memories of going to Windsor as very small child. My father took me, my brother and sister on Saturday mornings to see the changing of the guard. I can vividly remember watching the military brass band leave the castle, and as they marched off through the town we used to run through the cobbled streets behind the town hall to see them for a second time as they marched back to their barracks. If we had been well behaved dad might take us back to a toy shop in Maidenhead and add to our collection of toy soldiers. In the 1970s dad was working in Windsor making polythene bags, and it was always exciting going across to the factory when we were occasionally allowed. We even got to meet Father Christmas at the children's party they laid on each year. In 1977 Maidenhead Town Youth, my local boys' football club I played for, was chosen to take part in the Queen's Silver Jubilee celebrations in Windsor, which meant going on a float through the town during the day, and then lining the long walk in Windsor Great Park at night with torches as the Queen lit a massive bonfire. In 1983 I played football in goal for Windsor & Eton Youth for a year and we got to play in the FA Youth Cup against Wimbledon. We matched them for 45 minutes with the game standing 1-1 at half-time, but fitness and class won out in the second half as they ran riot running away 7-1 winners, but nevertheless it was still a great experience. When I first started to work in the family business we supplied the Crown Estate black rubbish bags delivered to the maintenance department located within the castle grounds, which meant we entered through the famous gated entrance and drove up to the round tower in order to deliver the bags. Security was somewhat more lax back then with just one policeman on the gate casting a cursory glance over the vehicle and the paperwork.

Windsor Castle dates back to medieval times. It was built by William the Conqueror after the Norman invasion, and has been used by a succession of monarchs dating back to Henry I. Today it is very much a working castle employing more than five hundred people. For some time I had wanted to photograph the castle at night, as the round tower is beautifully lit up at that time. I parked my car outside Windsor & Eton Riverside station on double yellow lines, and set up my tripod. I experimented with the shutter settings to get the best exposure possible, and I ended up using 4 seconds. This shows how important the tripod is, as it would have been impossible to have held the camera completely still for that period of time. I used a low 100 ISO setting to reduce noise in the photo and capture the castle in quite fine detail. I was really happy with this photo, as it turned out exactly as I hoped it would. Night time photography can be very rewarding, especially if you are prepared to plan the photo and I believe you get back what you put in.

26)   Ribblehead Viaduct

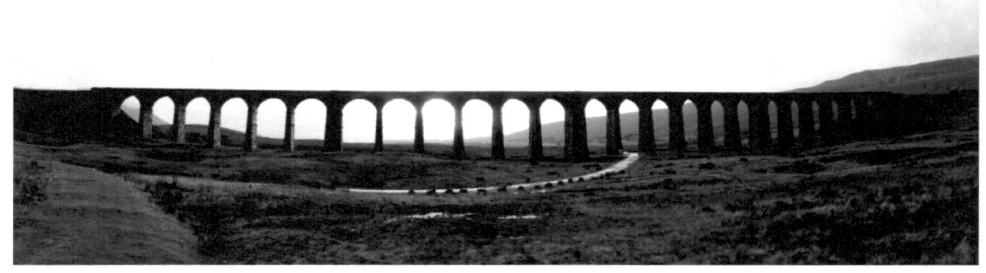

It is my brother who is the one in the family who has always had a love of railways, train-spotting from an early age and he would travel all over the country during his teenage years following this hobby. Being the younger brother I was drawn into this to a lesser degree, but occasionally I would go on some of these trips with him. I have always been more interested in the historical aspect and the architecture, particularly the engineering skills required to construct the British railway network including the bridges and tunnels. For me some of the constructions are truly amazing. The Ribblehead Viaduct in North Yorkshire is 400 metres long and 32 metres above the valley below at its highest point. The viaduct is the longest and most famous along the Settle to Carlisle railway. Work began in 1870, and four years later, in 1874, the viaduct was complete, having used an amazing one and a half million bricks. More poignantly over one hundred construction workers were killed, and in fact such was the extent of this that the railway company paid for the local graveyard to be extended. It is easy to forget in this modern era when safety is paramount the price paid by so many people constructing our nation's heritage.

It was a bitterly cold November afternoon when I took this photo, or what in actual fact were 3 photos taken using the panoramic setting on my camera. The viaduct is too wide to photograph at close range, so I took the photo in sections, and then used photo editing software to seamlessly stitch the pictures together into one panoramic picture. I converted it into black and white as it not only captures the bleak landscape, but the stunning beauty of the viaduct.

27)   Derwentwater

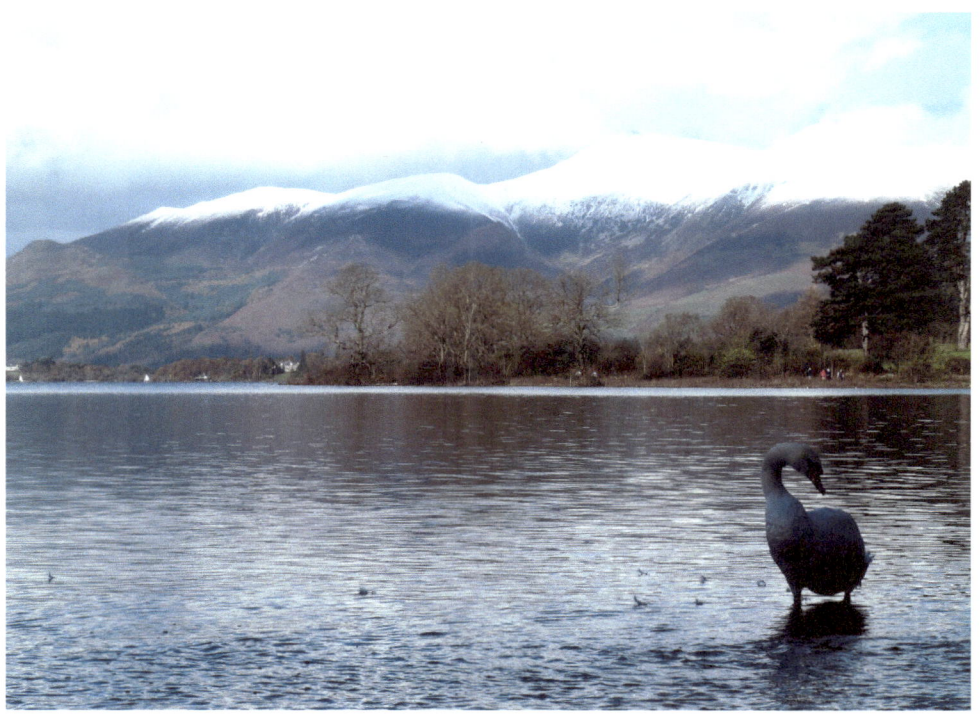

I spent a weekend in Cumbria in November 2012, which gave me the opportunity to visit the Lake District for the first time in almost 30 years. The last time I was there I went with my father, and this made this recent trip somewhat poignant. During the 1980s my parents would regularly travel up to see friends who had relocated from owning The Bird In Hand pub in Knowl Hill to taking over The Snooty Fox in Kirkby Lonsdale. On this recent trip I took my mother up to see these same friends. I find it interesting that the lifelong friendships my parents enjoyed remain as strong today as ever, and I can only hope that mine do likewise. When my father started the family business he had a customer in Windermere so he would use it as an excuse to travel up north and combine business with pleasure, and I made the trip with him a couple of times. On the first occasion we went with some of his old Maidenhead Rowing Club crowd and they were a very eccentric bunch indeed. On the second occasion I spent my 17th birthday there with my dad, and my brother who came across from

Leeds University to meet us. Unfortunately I had suffered a kidney illness two months earlier, which meant I was not joining them in a celebratory beer or two. In fact I ended up missing half the Easter term at school so this trip would have been just before I returned to my studies. On those trips we would cover an awful lot of miles, and I do regret not really fully appreciating the amazing scenery back then. Maybe this is an age thing? On the recent visit I was totally mesmerised the whole time, coming across one stunning location after another. My mother had recently discovered an old photo of me and my father together in the Lake District, which was somewhat remarkable as I developed a real aversion to having my picture taken in my teenage years. I think it was partly seeing this photo that gave me the idea to make the recent trip, and also that made me reflect on the past too.

On the day of photographing the Lakes the first snows of autumn had fallen, which added to the beautiful scenery. I wanted to cover as many locations as possible as I only had one day there. I managed to cover the lakes of Grasmere, Thirlmere, Derwentwater, Buttermere, Crummock and Ullswater along with the Honister and Whinlatter passes. Parking was an issue and so at scene of the photo I joined the National Trust. This not only solved the immediate parking problem, but also opens up a whole new world of opportunities for days out in 2013.

The photograph was taken at Derwentwater which was breathtaking. I was able to walk right down to the water and play around with my camera. I am not sure where the swan actually came from as it wasn't there when I arrived, but it adds something to the picture. The picture encompasses everything about the region: a wonderful lakeside location, stunning mountain ranges with a touch of nature thrown in. All I did with the photo was to tweak the brightness and contrast.

28)   Red Balloon

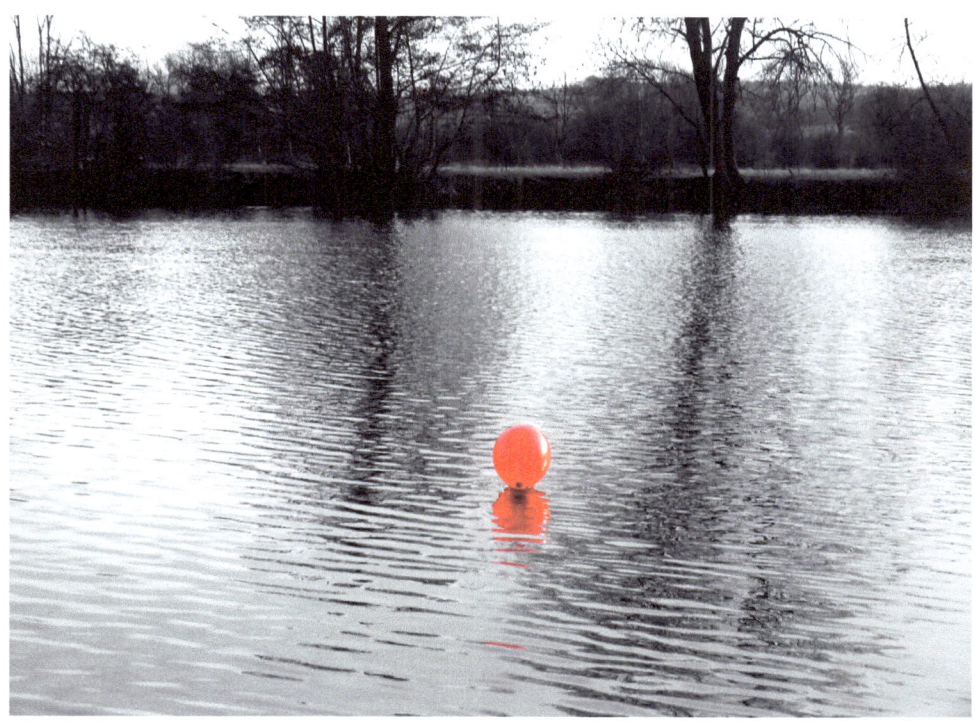

Working so close to the river Thames in the Buckinghamshire countryside with its stunning scenery has some advantages. Firstly it can be a great place to get away from the everyday stresses of work and to clear your head. Secondly though as for an enthusiastic amateur photographer it offers endless photographic opportunities. The idea behind this photo was simply to represent the colour red. I immediately decided to go down a selective photo colour route where all other colours bar red would be turned into black and white allowing the red to stand out as the dominant colour in the photo. There are many software programs available that can isolate colours and the software I use is Tinsii. My original ideas included red letter boxes and the traditional red telephone box. Letter boxes in particular interested me as sometimes they are built into buildings and as a result stand out well. I soon came round to the idea of using red balloons. The challenge was then to find a location. I had grand designs of going up to London to one of the bridges over The Thames and dropping a load of balloons and then taking as many photos from different positions as possible before the tide took them away.

I settled in the end on the village of Medmenham close to work, and so was able to spend a bit of time setting up the tripod and trying out a few ideas. In one photo I wore a red football shirt and used the timer to capture myself throwing red balloons into the air. However in the end I came back to my love of water and used the water as a very effective prop. The idea was to set the balloon off on its own journey, which also symbolises the journey I feel I have been on in recent years. As in life you can chart the start of a voyage but sometimes where it will end is not always as easy to know. I had trouble getting balloons into the full stream and many got stuck in the reeds, which also made for quite good photos. Eventually one balloon broke free and moved into the main flow of the river achieving a perfect photographic position for me. Once I had used the software to isolate the red balloon I sharpened the image and tweaked the brightness and contrast to get the final effect. I think the image captures "red" and has enough there to grab and perhaps hold the viewer's attention.

29)   The Rule of Thirds

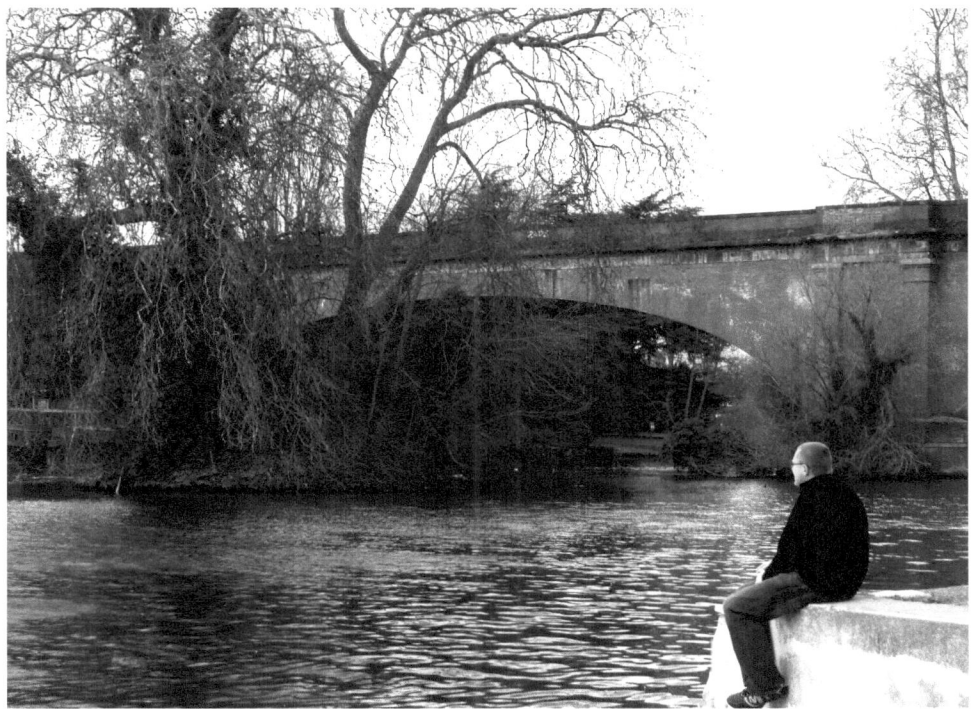

This winter scene is on the river Thames at Maidenhead with the Brunel railway bridge with its huge famous sounding arches spanning the river. As young children Dad would take me, my brother and sister most Sunday lunchtimes to Maidenhead Rowing Club located just the other side of the railway bridge where his old rowing colleagues met up. The original idea behind this photograph was to illustrate the Rule of Thirds photography technique. I applied the rule twice on this photo. The water line was a natural line for the bottom third of the photo, and by placing myself in the picture I put myself in the right hand bottom third by using a tripod and timer. I quite liked this touch as it wasn't intended to be a portrait, but by putting myself in the photo it kind of opens up the rest of the photo and gives a good sense of scale with the bridge in the background.

30) A Musical Journey

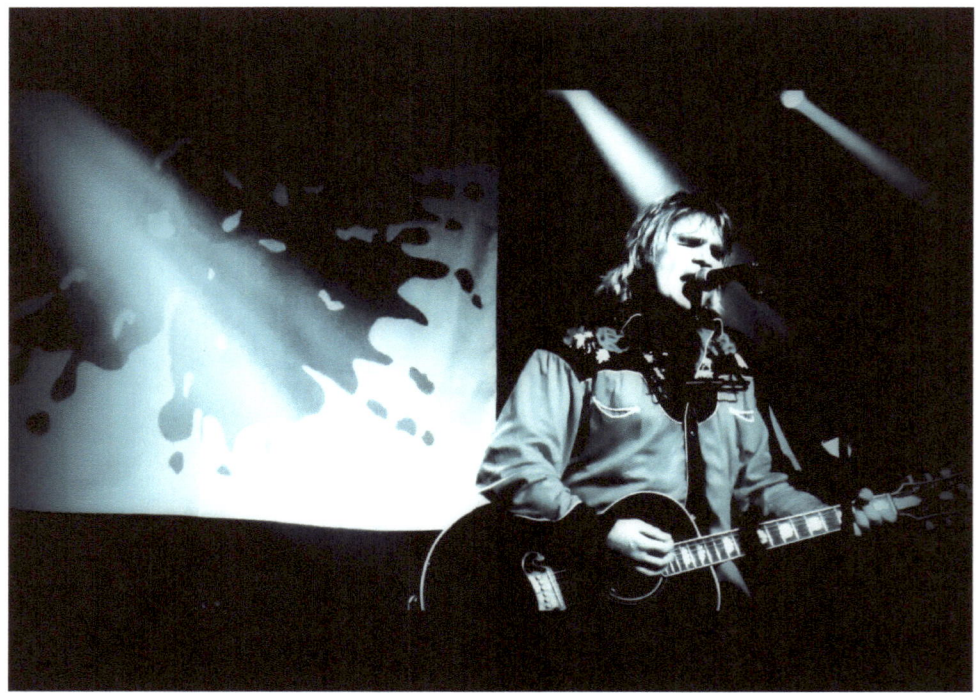

Music has always played a huge part in my life, and The Alarm is my favourite band of all time. I have followed them for nearly 30 years and their music is everything I like music to be. I first heard them back in 1983 when I was seventeen listening to John Peel on my little radio in my bedroom when I heard this wonderfully powerful acoustic stomping tune called "The Stand", which was the third single by them. I ordered the 7" and 12" singles from my local record shop in Maidenhead and for the only time in my life I took records into school to play to my friends once they arrived. On the basis of that, four of us went up to see the band play at The Marquee in London in May 1983. I was blown away by these weird-looking band members with spiky hair banging out tunes on acoustic guitars with such power and energy, the like of which I had never seen before. Over the following months I went to see the band in London at every opportunity and saw just the most amazing shows. We missed last trains home, got stuck in car parks and went to venues I never knew existed. The old ballroom venues in London were simply magical. The band for me was at their best playing live and studio recordings sometimes never quite captured the essence of those live gigs. I remember in May 1985 going to see the band play at the Hammersmith Odeon direct from watching Arsenal play away at West Brom, and then outside the gig afterwards I saw my hero Charlie Nicholas leave so I chased him down the road to sign my football programme from that day. I saw them support Queen at Wembley in 1986 and then U2 at the Cardiff Arms Park in 1987. I remember the Wembley show mainly as shortly before The Alarm came on stage we made our way down to the front having to step over loads of picnics that the Queen fans had laid out for the day. Cardiff was very eventful as having got the train down to Cardiff we had a quite a few drinks in the bars around the stadium. On entering the stadium to my horror they were not selling alcohol and the only drink on sale was Panda Pops! I was tempted to leave there and then and get a train home. Fortunately both The Alarm and U2 were amazing and it was a wonderful day. The original line-up disbanded in 1991 and I think it was no coincidence that I spent the next ten years in relative musical retirement not going to many gigs and I just tended to buy CDs rather than going to see bands play live. However when Mike Peters put a new line-up together and started playing as The Alarm again I suddenly started going back to see live once more.

When Mike Peters played the Oxford Academy in November 2012, which was coming up to thirty years for me following his music, I decided for the very first time to try and photograph him. I took both my compact digital and SLR cameras to the gig, and the only pre-conceived idea that I had was to try and capture a sense of a musician playing with the passion and emotion that has been a feature of his performances over the years. I found the whole experience of photographing in a dimly lit auditorium very challenging and rather surprisingly I got better results with my little compact camera. I found many settings either left the photos flat and lifeless or - if I went for a longer shutter exposure - the image ended up blurred. I played with the various settings on both cameras and eventually got the best result on the compact using a candle-light portrait setting it had. The first adjustment in editing the photo was adding a little warmth to it and a hint of soft focus. I used the cinemascope setting to add a more dramatic letter box style, converted the photo into black and white with a

Holga-ish effect and finally used a blue tint. It is the kind of photo I could see being used in promotional literature.

***** THE END *****

Epilogue

In September 2012 my mother underwent major surgery to remove the cancerous tumour from her bowel. Prior to the surgery we were warned that there was the possibility that she might be in intensive care for 24 hours after surgery. It was a long day spent waiting for news and the ward was unable to give us any kind of update which only added to our already fraught nerves. Finally at 6:00 in the evening we given the news that mum was back on the ward. Me, my brother and sister went over the hospital expecting to find a very poorly and drowsy patient post operation. We were very surprised to find mum sitting up and talking nineteen to the dozen.

Her recovery from surgery in the early stages was pretty amazing to observe, and the biggest frustration for mum has been the retraining of her bowel, which still doesn't always behave itself as she might like. It has to be said that she is not the most patient of patients when it comes to taking things easy during the recovery and rehabilitation period. In the scheme of things though this is a small price to pay. The surgery has without doubt saved her life and we are in debt to all the doctors and nurses in NHS who have been so wonderful in their care of mum and putting her on the road to full fitness.

www.ingramcontent.com/pod-product-compliance
Lightning Source LLC
Chambersburg PA
CBHW041108180526
45172CB00001B/162